Invocations

to the

Light

WISTANCIA STONE

BLUE DOLPHIN
PUBLISHING

Published by
Blue Dolphin Publishing, Inc.
P.O. Box 8, Nevada City, CA 95959
Orders: 1-800-643-0765
Web site: http://www.bluedolphinpublishing.com

ISBN: 1-57733-011-0

Library of Congress Cataloging-in-Publication Data

Stone, Wistancia, 1947–
    Invocations to the light / Wistanica Stone.
        p.   cm.
    ISBN 1-57733-011-0
    1. I AM Religious Activity Prayer—books and
devotions—English.   2. Spiritual life—I AM Religious
activity.   I. Title.
BP605.I18S76 1999
299'.93—dc21   99-25878
                                                    CIP

Cover art: Lito Castro

Printed in the United States of America

10   9   8   7   6   5   4   3   2   1

Invocations
to the
Light

Mother Mary

St. Germain

Lord Sananda

Kwan Yin

Master Kuthumi

Dedication

*W*E CHOSE TO COME FORTH from Source—the Formless—and entered the world of Form. We are hybrids of both. Within each of us lies the bridge between the two. Deep within the heart is a flame, the same element and quality of Father/Mother God. This book is dedicated to the Oneness in All Life and to bridging Heaven and Earth within each human heart.

May the words contained here be used as stepping stones for many bridges as we awaken to the vastness of our being, reminding us of the power that lies within our own silent sanctuaries. As we link with Divine Beings and our Higher Selves, may we heal our feelings of separation and come softly into reunion with Source and our own Grand Selves.

In deepest love and gratitude, this book is dedicated to the Inner Plane Cosmic and Planetary Ascended Masters who reach out in love to humankind and to Earth to heal, harmonize, awaken and lift consciousness. Deep exaltations and appreciation go to the Archangels and Angels who carry their radiance to us straight from the heart of Source. Through their resonance and overlighting, they are indeed illuminating our pathway Home. Blessings to Mother Earth for supporting us all through many incarnations as we endeavor to remember who we are.

This book is offered to the Source of all Creation, to All That Is. Not only did You place within us a spark of Your Divine Energy—a piece of You containing Love, Wisdom and Power—You also provided us with a means to feel and know that miracle with our open hearts. As if that were not enough, You surrounded us with Spiritual Overseers to protect and guide us; beings who can become our dearest companions if we invite them into our lives. As we share ourselves with them, they share themselves with us; if we look deeply enough, we see that we are all connected.

We are all One and all part of You. Only through the experience of You can we see ourselves for who *we* truly are. We are ONE. Only then can we solve the mystery of The One and the Many and know our place in the Divine Plan.

I dedicate this book to this Truth—that there is only One. And to the Divine paradox whereby we call to the many to assist us in anchoring, activating and actualizing our Ascension into Oneness.

Contents

Acknowledgments

With all of my love I wish to thank Mother/Father God for the many blessings of Life and Union. I can never thank You in words or even the outpourings of my heart. If, within the Language of Light, the vibrational spark I AM is a color, a tone, or a geometry—please play my tune, paint my color, breathe my lines deeper into Your Divine Plan and weave my pattern into Your Heart forevermore. May the words of my mouth and the meditations of my heart be always in acknowledgment of You!

For their inspiration, radiance, and constant assistance, I thank the many Masters and Angels of the Cosmic and Planetary Hierarchies for overlighting me during the writing of this book and in my life. You have become my essential and dearest, most trusted companions. Your guidance is always given when I turn within inside to ask.

I am especially grateful to Lord Sananda, The Divine Mother, Archangels Michael and Faith, Metatron and Melchizedek. Only now do I see how The Divine

Mother embraced me with Love Divine since the beginning of my spiritual creation. Mother of all Mothers, I find my Peace, my Rest in You.

How many eons have I been under the Divine Universal tutelage of you, Lord Melchizedek? You mirror Eternity to me.

Metatron, I cannot fathom your pattern of life and yet I know you play a part in the definition of my Destiny. You enliven each cell with circuitry from your Great Electronic Presence.

Archangels Michael and Faith, you were the first archangels that came through my channel. While I cannot glimpse the radius of your radiance, I have known you to Empower my Will and help me to remove illusions and obstacles, restoring my Faith. In truth, you saw the angel in me, pulled out the stiff wings and taught me to fly.

Beloved Lord Sananda—you are Bliss to me and I Am an extention of your breath. First you taught me, day and night, to open the heart and explore the inner chambers. Eternal moments you have placed your hand on my heart and breathed upon the door. You knocked with me and the pathways were opened. You stood at every fork of every road, beckoning the Christ in me to keep coming and to stand up and speak. You overshadowed me through tears and laughter—the Dark Nights of the Soul and the triumphs of initiation—reminding me: that we are One. We have the same Mother and Father. The golden table was set and victory assured.

You have acknowledged Christ and God in me—I acknowledge you now as real and as constant as Breath!

I thank Sabrina, the very first angel that I came into communion with.

I thank Maharaji, my first Earth Master, who is known as a Perfect Master or one who teaches "perfection." You revealed the ancient Knowledge of direct God-experience within and I thank you for placing me firmly on my path 20 years ago.

I acknowledge the tremendous amount of love, support, and vision of my editor, Michelle Hausmann, whose talents tied this volume together.

I thank Jeannie for telling me that, since invocations are such a strong force in my life, I should put them in a book.

And last, but not least, I thank my Golden Retriever Brianna and my cat, Mushroom, for their unconditional love and patience with me when I am too busy to play,

An Invocation for This Book

I request a blessing from Father-Mother-God-Source to be deeply present in my heart. Help me be a vehicle for assisting others in the use of the tool of invocation.

I ask that this book be overlit by Masters and Angels, those infinite numbers of Beings of Light and Love directly linked with The Creator who are ready to assist humankind in the evolvement of our vast potential as Divine Beings living on Earth. Let it be a call for help in lifting humankind and Earth into our ascension into greater light and knowingness.

As this book is used, let it be one stepping stone among many on the pathway to mastery of the Self. Anoint these pages with light sufficient to begin the action of reclaiming gifts and abilities of our divine nature. Let each page carry light to ignite the God flame in the heart.

From my heart, I send forth the image of invocations as crystal butterflies carrying and depositing Light into the World of Form. Let the *understanding emerge that* WE *are Divine Beings and that as we uncover the memory and mystery of who and what we are, we too shall emerge as our Radiant Selves bearing great light.*

May these crystal butterflies multiply throughout the Universe and be seen, heard, and known as Heaven on Earth is re-created....

Amen

Introduction

$\mathscr{It}$ is the way of the Creation to reach up to where help resides and call it down to where it is needed. As Earth citizenry presently, we see examples of this exchange all around us. When we want a guide to help us through unfamiliar terrain, we hire someone who knows the area. Teachers are the guides that help us with subjects that we want or need to learn. To be helped is to be taught and cared for by others higher up on the rungs of understanding. Once we advance our understanding, we turn and share it with others thus taking on the role of teacher and contributing to the process of overall growth. We become agents of change.

We were taught that our world is three dimensional. The height, width, and depth of what we perceive is how our environment is understood. We can see, feel, taste, smell, and hear these dimensions. We have relied on these primary physical senses to identify the space we occupy; sensory feedback assures us our existence within third dimensional consciousness.

Beyond the third dimension of most people's experience exists numbers of other dimensions, dimensions that scientists are just beginning to acknowledge and of which intuitives have always known. The fourth dimension, for instance, is perceivable through intuition causing us to know certain things without tangible proof. An awareness of non-apparent (by the five senses) occurrences and energies is a *fourth* dimensional consciousness and allows some comprehension of a certain level of spiritual presence.

It is believed that dimensions are differentiated by energy frequency and light reflection. That is easy to comprehend when considering the three planes that define familiar third dimension, but it becomes more complicated when attempting to conceive of higher dimensions. Beyond the third dimension exists ever increasing frequencies that define the "stages" on which beings of a higher resonance exist. The higher the frequency, the higher and faster the vibration of those who reside there. As vibration increases, so does the capacity to hold light. As more light is held, the closer to the Source of Creation each being moves. Light is attainable through the higher expressions of love, wisdom, and power.

Many people are stepping into the truth that we and our world—everything— is made of light. Scientists agree that when the smallest atom is broken apart, energy pours out in the form of light. As light, we have the opportunity to shine brightly or dimly. As consciousness, we have the choice to embrace expansion, or to remain in fear and limitation. We are Light Beings living in the World of Form—particles of Original Source seeking vastness in experience. We are drawn "upward" to where the light is brightest in search of our God Selves.

The truth is that we are much more than our physical selves; we consist of many bodies of light, in ascending order, much like a cross-section of a great tree. Simply put, there are many levels to what is referred to as our Higher Self, including a Christed Overself and an individuated God Presence referred to as the Mighty I Am Presence. Who we really are is already vast and has always been so, for we are, in truth, part of the Eternal Self—the one Great Group Being we call God.

Invocations are a tool to awaken a connection to our True Selves. When we embark on the journey toward this Truth, invocations become instruments of empowerment to serve the vastness of our experience. Invocations enable us to amass supportive energy from higher dimensions in order to co-create for the highest good. Like prayer and meditation, invocations inspire, awaken, teach, and add to the light we carry into the world. With invocations, we become magnets pulling light toward ourselves which, in turn, causes us to feel more joy, wisdom, harmony, purpose, energy, creativity, and love. In invoking the help and guidance of higher beings, we reach up to where the *help resides and bring it down to where help is needed...*

Invocations are an action of reaching "up," but the action is actually twofold. Though we are reaching "up" toward spiritual Masters and Angels, we are simultaneously reaching into our own hearts where Source exists inside of us. When we invoke, we purify our environment and ourselves and open to receiving guidance, love, and energy from the higher dimensions. The act of invocation raises our consciousness.

When we call the names of God and the Masters and Angels, we connect to Source unfolding into Creation. In doing so we become an active part of the Creation process as it seeks its ultimate expression. Calling upon the pure formless energy of Source, via the stepdown transformers of Divine Energy—Divine Beings—we imbue Creation itself with even greater possibilities, adding our love to the whole.

In invoking the assistance of higher beings, we are invoking Source (God) within us to be better known. We are reawakening that part of ourselves already in harmony and balance with the Masters; indeed the *Master* within us. We are asking to recognize our part in the Divine Plan, and to move through our experience with optimal grace. As Source is evoked from within, we rise up to meet Its love and find our happiness, our fulfillment, our purpose. The endless questions are answered and we can move forward in knowingness.

When the call is made in sincerity, the answer comes. The answer is the knowledge of Source, the connection to Source, the peace of Source. In our efforts to merge with The Source/The One, we diminish the pain of separation from the Creator or any other beloved. We hear Source singing to us, "Come back to Me, come into the awareness of love. Fill yourself up with Me. Take My Love into yourself first, then pour My Love into Creation so that all may expand in Light. I, too, expand."

Through invocations we sing, "Help me heal the separation that I feel so I can come back Home. Familiarize me again with the vibration of perfect love. Help me to receive Source and to know the Light that never fails. Help me to come back into deeper and deeper levels of consciousness. Help me to come back into the One Great Heart. To relieve all suffering which stems forth from separation and to come into the experience of oneness."

It is intended that we show you a new, yet ancient, way of expressing your Self. The experience of this book is meant to be a leaping off point for your own creativity in invoking the blessings you need in your life. As you delve deeper into your creative heart, the Invocations of Light will come bubbling forth and you will discover a great camaraderie with wonderful Beings. Use your power, your voice, your heart, to call the Love and Light of Spirit to work with you in these times of personal and planetary expansion

As you begin, we encourage you to skip around, back and forth to your heart's content. Hopefully, this book will get very well-used and become like the *Velveteen Rabbit* whose ears and fur became rubbed off by love. It would be good if the pages all got a bit crumpled and worn. We have provided you with extra space to fill with your own inspirations, your own invocations, if you wish. Each heart has its own manner of calling, allow yours to sing out!

Life is the love story of each heart—Invocations are the love song....

−1−

Reaching for the Light

*I*NVOCATION IS A SACRED ACT. Some personal preparation to bring you into sacred space is important for
it to be the powerful tool of transformation that it is.
Remember, the heart is the gateway—or *stargate*—to
feeling the sacred unity of life. So access the heart. Begin
by connecting to Source in whatever way you can. Be
aware that intention is a dynamic tool to manifest a
linking with Source. Be present in respect, in faith, in
sincerity. Ask for these virtues if you need to.

Take a moment to center yourself. Visualize white
and golden light encompassing you. You can say to
yourself, "I surround myself with peace, love, and light,
and create a sheath of protection around myself." You
may choose to outpicture platinum light—a frequency
above the gold. Take a few slow, deep breaths and
release the tension out of your body. Each breath is a
new gift of life—the Masters call it a "new morning."

1

And with every in-breath and out-breath there is a point of stillness which brings serenity when it is your focus. Feel the finer energies around you. Feel your heart and connect with your breath. You may wish to visualize a "figure eight" connecting your breath with your heart so they are joined and begin to intertwine. It is like breathing through the heart. From your heart, breathe light into the rest of your body. Feel the top of your head—your crown—and consciously *intend* it to open to bring light from the higher dimensions into the physical, emotional, mental, and etheric layers of your Being.

Ground yourself by directing a ray of your own light from the heart down into the center of the planet, anchoring it to the crystal that lies deep within the center of Earth. Then send another beam of light into Heaven or God or the Great Central Sun (whatever feels right for you). Take a moment to breathe and *feel* the returning of these energies back into the heart from above and from below you. You are the bridge connecting Heaven and Earth.

The energy of life is Light. The energy that is called God is Light. The energy of the smallest atomic particle breaking apart is Light. All is Light—know that this is a scientific and spiritual truth. Embrace the paradox that you express yourself as a separate entity, yet hold within your consciousness the deep reality that there is a Oneness of which you are a part. Though it may seem that Divine Beings whose guidance and help you seek dwell in another reality, they are a part of the Oneness, too. There is no separation between yourself and the Oneness. The sense that you are alone is an illusion.

As you speak invocations, notice how you feel, how the space around you feels. You will probably be aware of an increase in energy, both in yourself and in the space you occupy. These energies may be felt in many different ways such as a sense of warmth, tingling, or a buzzing. Perhaps you may feel like a bottle being filled up with a liquid or a balloon being filled with air. You may feel larger than usual, full of power, like "more of yourself." The atmosphere in the room will change as the energies that you call forth draw nearer. With clairvoyant sight, interplays of light and color can be seen. The important thing is to feel the love that will invariably fill your heart. Your energy will begin to come into resonance with the energies that have been invoked. When the invocation has been made and the energies have been summoned by love, it is easier for the heart to come into the vibration of love. Feel at ease with your own experience and know that it will also change as your awareness of the new energies expands.

Consciously Qualify the Energy—Be Specific

There are a couple of important points to remember when invoking the assistance of Divine Beings. To begin with, be specific about whose assistance you are calling on. Although you may feel protected, generally, from forces that are of a dim light, there are still many negative extraterrestrials and astral entities, for example, who move about this plane observing and playing tricks on others. Some entities look for vulnerability and a chance to elicit light from a lightbearer.

It is always best not to say simply, "Help me!" Be specific about the beings you are wanting assistance from. Call forth for the help you truly seek and that call will compel the answer. For example, "Lord Sananda, please overlight me." "Archangel Faith, please help me to restore my faith!" "Michael, protect me!" "Mother Mary, be with me in this hour. I need your loving-kindness."

Close the Invocation

It is also important to close the invocation with a seal. What you are actually doing is sealing the energy. The most common way in which to close an invocation is with the word "Amen," which means "Aum." You will feel the difference in energy when you complete an invocation. It serves as a word of thanks, an indication to the Masters invoked that you are now concluding the invocation, as well as an energetic seal that closes off the power that is inherent in the request. It is like placing a period at the end of a sentence, marking the finish line. It is also an act of protection for the one who is making the call; no one else will be able to add to what has been already spoken and commanded into action.

Understand that invocations date back to ancient civilizations on Earth where they were common expressions in the temples of love and light. They hold a power within them. But know that Light forces as well as Dark forces can be invoked. Within this understanding it is always a good practice to complete one's invocation and be specific.

It is also best to learn the correct pronunciation of the names of the Masters, Cosmic Beings and Angels. In some traditions it is believed that naming a god or goddess incorrectly brings in but half of their energy. It is our intention to introduce invocations as a powerful and joyful experience. So let go of any timidity and always know that sincerity is the most important virtue. The sincere heart opens all doors and can do no wrong. Just come from the heart and speak with clarity, love, and power.

There is no right way or wrong way to invoke the assistance of Divine Beings other than coming from the heart and speaking with clarity. You are free to reach out in any manner that feels comfortable and appropriate. Submerging yourself in the beauty of the moment and coming from love for the highest good brings your will into alignment with Divine Will.

Though we have provided many invocations for you to read aloud, the best experience is to make up your own to meet your own needs as seen from your own heart. They may be written first and read, or spoken spontaneously. Keep in mind that words are an energy—there is great power in the spoken word.

After calling, sit quietly and open to receiving. Know that you have been heard.

The Difference Between Invocation, Prayer,
& Meditation

Very simply, Prayer is talking to Source. Meditation is listening to Source and experiencing Source within. Invoking is co-creating with Source.

Prayer is coming to Source in passivity. It can be an expression of gratitude, or a sigh of "God, help me," like a child slipping its small hand into the hand of the parent. Carry me for awhile. Hold me. Love me. Help me. Fill me up and give me the strength to continue. Exquisite experiences can happen while sitting in the pool of prayer. It is powerful and life-changing.

Meditation is being *with* the vibration that sustains all of life and is within us. It is putting your attention on Source within and then releasing yourself into the *experience* of Source within. In the act of true meditation, the mind's impressions are silenced and the "still small voice" can be experienced. That "still small voice" is the Imprint of Source upon you. This imprint will change you as the influence of Source removes Karma and shows you truths where only illusions and half-truths were before. Meditation is a "two-way prayer" wherein your heart unfolds in unspoken yearning and in turn beholds the answers, the enlightenment. These are given in the language of light which is beyond words. In the silence, it is love.

Invocation is the action of joining highest intention with the forces of God which can be your own individualized God Self or any number of Divine Beings whose service it is to aid in consciousness transformation. It is a means for rallying the strength and wisdom of enlightened beings from advanced dimensions to implement change for the highest good within any situation. Invocation calls forth the Angels and Inner Plane Masters who eagerly await an opportunity to help. It is bringing forth the *actual* and *true* energetic presence of an Angel or a Master to be instrumental in the holiness of a moment. It is a request for Their hands-on help to bring Light forward for a specific occasion, a specific challenge, activation, or divine dispensation.

Invocations are calls to *receive* in order to *give*. They are a natural movement of the receiving heart. We open to receive more light in order to give more light. We call to receive from the reservoirs of light and love in Heaven in order to flood the Earth and our lives with higher vibrations and higher knowingness therein creating Heaven on Earth. This is the essence of Ascension into the Light, or spiritual evolution. It is, essentially, Life fulfilling its two basic movements: magnetizing and radiating, giving and receiving. Invocations lift everything into the perfected state.

As an invocation is put forth from your purity and innocence, *you* are empowered to create the needed changes along with the other forces that have stepped forward at your request. There enjoins a co-creation to move the moment toward its finest expression, its fullest potential of goodness. You open a doorway for the Light to cascade down upon the space you occupy and it enriches the experience, elevating it to its greatest potential.

Invocation is an ancient form of empowering the Self to rise out of the clay of lower consciousness. It was a part of the great mysteries of forgotten civilizations, references to which often reside in mythology and esoteric literature. Within the reality of reincarnation, there are many who feel a certain familiarity to its practice.

Invocation diminishes the fear that we are alone and forces the ego to still its incessant chatter long enough for truth to emerge about the nature of our being. We are beautiful creatures searching for the love and wisdom to contribute our fullest selves to the unfoldment of Creation.

The heart knows what it wants and what it needs in order to grow. A Heart is like a thirsty flower, reaching to the sun for its lifeforce. A flower doesn't need to understand photosynthesis to partake of it; it just knows to raise its petals to receive the rays of the sun to sustain itself. Invocations are like opening your petals to God. The Sons and Daughters of God open to receive from the God-Parents—the Divine Father Principle of Power and Divine Mother Principle of Love.

All three tools—Meditation, Prayer, and Invocation—are means to awaken and experience the peace and love of the Creator and thereby know ourselves as sparks of that Light. Understanding the difference enables us to know when and how to use each of them.

They are not substitutes for one another; they complement each other. These are tools for our enlightenment and ascension into greater awareness and greater levels of Light and Love.

Whose Help Do We Reach for on the Higher Dimensions?

We seek the heart of God. As beings living on Earth, we can call upon the Spiritual Hierarchy for Earth. We contact the help of the Archangels and their legions of Angels. We may summon our own Guardian Angels— both the ones that were assigned to us at birth and ones we may have picked up along the way—or the Beloved Ascended Masters who, in their love and service to the Earth, remain within our reach. There are numerous Divine Beings who work in a cosmic capacity to expand God-consciousness. We also may communicate with higher aspects of ourselves, including the I Am Presence or monad, which is the individualized God-Self in which is contained all perfection, wisdom, and love.

When we really open up to the reality of existence, we will see that even planets and galaxies are *conscious beings*. We can call to the consciousness of the Sun, as well as the consciousness of the cells in our very own divine bodies. All life is connected and accessible through invocations.

As You Begin the Practice of Invocation,
the Following Points May Help

  &so; *Our Free Will is honored by Divine Beings.*

  &so; *They wait for our calls for assistance.*

  &so; *We gain clarity when we state our intention.*

  &so; *We learn the balance of Surrender and Command.*

  &so; *We feel a part of the Oneness of Life.*

  &so; *We become Co-creators with God and the Masters*
and recognize our unity with all life.

  &so; *We feel the effects, changes, blessings of*
that which is invoked.

  &so; *We feel the presence of those whom we invoke.*

  &so; *We serve the process of Creation by consciously*
participating in its unfoldment.

  &so; *We discover our great potential;*
we wake up and remember who we are.

–2–

Ask For
What You
Want and Need

Calling out to the higher dimensions is like holding up your little cup and letting a great pitcher of a very clear sparkling elixir fill it to overflowing. Your cup can and will runneth over. In the Invocations provided, we have many "elixirs" from which to choose. They can be used for the physical body, emotional body, mental body, etheric body, and spiritual bodies. Use them to improve the quality of your life psychologically, physically and spiritually.

Ask and you shall receive. There is nothing that we cannot ask for and there is nothing that will be withheld as long as it is in Divine Order and within Divine Timing for the Highest Good. Our job is to *ask*. Begin by asking for an open heart with which to embrace the gifts that will be offered.

Understand Your Role, Your Purpose, Your Calling in This Lifetime

Those in the higher dimensions working for Earth and Her resident beings are devoted to moving you into the next level of your evolution. Showing you the way to your true role in the Divine Plan is uppermost on the Angelic agenda. Their loving guidance comes to you subtly through a shift in yearnings, new dreams/visions and ideas, surprising coincidences, and the whisper in your mind that you did not consciously compose. Those in the Higher Dimensions long to raise you up to participate in God's design as was intended in the blueprint of your soul. To understand your blueprint, to see your vision and purpose become manifest, call out in invocation to be shown the way. Be open to the Presence of the Angels and Masters in your life.

Inspire Yourself and Others to Positive Action

You will find, as you submerge yourself in the action of invocation, inspiration will follow. It is through this inspiration that your greatest works may be found. Whatever your God-given talents and abilities, the inspiration to move with them toward productive outcome is imminent using invocation as a personal tool. Many are already opening up to the presence of Angels and Masters in their lives. Many hold much light from this opening. In this light, inspiration abounds.

Find Personal Empowerment

As we call the Masters and Angels into the openness of our hearts, their company brings the Law of Resonance to us. As insight, wisdom, and love grow, we begin to resonate with the vibration of the Masters, becoming masters ourselves. When we place our attention on the Light, the Light is amplified and anchored within our bodies. As we focus on the highest, our focus brings us a new vision. It has a snowballing effect. Invoke, invoke, invoke and you experience, experience, experience. As you invoke more, you experience more, and as you receive more, you can give more. It is that simple.

Know That You Are Not Alone

Invocations affirm that we are connected in a great web of consciousness. That we, too, are Spiritual beings currently experiencing a physical body. We can feel the Presence that is our longing and is our need. We can stand in unity with the rest of creation and ask for blessings and ask for *Now*. We have been feeling separation from our hearts, our Higher Selves, our purpose, and our Source for so long that many of us believe that separation is the way of life. There is, however, another way—Oneness and Union within the brilliance of all Creation.

Find Healing

What are we healing? We are healing our feelings of separation from Source. If you are physically in perfect health and know not *who* and *what* you are, you still need healing. True healing is healing our experiences, feelings, illusions and belief systems of separation from God. When we heal this separation we come into the Radiant Self. The Christ is Blossoming within us. We ascend into a higher consciousness. We will have healed and will have come back *consciously* into Source. We will be available to help others come Home.

−3−

Fourteen Archangels
& Seven Primary Rays
of Creation

CREATION IS MADE UP OF ENERGY which is seen as light. Even in the denseness of physical expression, we know that colors emerge as light dividing and combining to reflect our world back to us. Color has meaning in the impression it leaves. In the experience of the third dimension, many colors have mysteriously taken on personalities, even though the meaning is not yet understood. Pink is feminine and the color of love. Boys and many third dimension agents of power are dressed in blue. Purple denotes royalty. Gold has always been a splendid color symbolizing prominence. Platinum is beyond gold—denoting riches and excellence.

In the upper dimensions, color has great significance as well. The frequency that is associated with a particular color is a direct extension of Source and represents specific Divine virtues. As Beings of Light,

15

Divine Beings emanate rays of color unique to individual intent and function within the unfoldment of Creation. These colors are referred to as the Rays of Creation, and in our Invocations we will be using these Light Rays, or Flames, to augment the process and enhance both the experience and the results we are seeking.

Angels are divine intelligence in action. Though there are many, many angelic beings concerned with Earth and each one of us, we are going to concentrate on *Archangels* for our purposes in this chapter. Archangels are pure and perfect Beings of Light who serve God in a cosmic capacity and are of the highest order of the Angelic Kingdom working with form. In general, they emanate a particular God-virtue and represent one of the seven main Rays of Creation.

There are fourteen primary Archangels—seven masculine and seven feminine—assigned to work with Earth and her citizens at this time. They are: Michael and Faith, Jophiel and Constance (also known as Christine), Chamuel and Charity, Raphael and Mother Mary, Uriel and Aurora Grace, and Zadkiel and Amethyst. *Though each has specific areas of intent, they are also interchangeable. They may be called upon as a group or individually.*

The action of a Light Ray or Ray of Creation brings God principles into manifestation in the world of Form.

ॐ

Gifts from God enter our world through these Rays.

❧

The Seven Rays represent
Seven major developmental phases of unfolding life.
Each Ray has a color and two Archangels
associated with it
Each Archangel, in turn, creates legions of angels
of that specific ray and intent.
The colors of the rays may differ
from one tradition or teaching to another.
This is because there are esoteric and exoteric colors.
At the Archangelic level
it is the esoteric "color" that is perceived.

❧

The Seven principle feelings required for mastery on Earth
are represented by the seven main Archangels—
masculine and feminine.

Within these pages, we will focus on the seven planetary and more familiar rays that are influencing the Earth at this time and their usefulness in invocations; however it is to be noted that, as of this writing, significant changes are occurring and are forthcoming in our overall experience such that transformation has moved us into octaves much higher than seven. There are now Cosmic Rays and higher expressions of the Rays that can be invoked. That will, however, be for a subsequent book.

As more energy, light, and assistance come to Earth and to Earth's residents—and as we and our planet move intentionally onto a pathway of ascension or escalation into higher frequencies of light—more people will be experiencing changes to what is currently accepted as the "norm." Among other things, our bodies are evolving into a multi-chakra system, well beyond the commonly known seven. As a counterpart to this phenomena, our DNA structure is becoming more complex and more highly geometrical.

Though we will only address the Seven Rays of Creation and their corresponding Angelic overseers for our purposes, know that we are all quickening and receiving within our awareness and/or into our fields of energy many higher dimensions, cosmic rays, and accelerated infusions of Light and blessings.

Archangel Michael & Archangel Faith

First Ray – Blue
Power, Divine Will, Faith, Protection

Archangel Michael is the Lord of the Archangels and Director of the Angelic Kingdom. He is referred to as the "Head or High Command," and is considered a trinitized expression of God along with Metatron and Melchizedek. His service, among others, is the restoration of spiritual realms. He is called the "Angel of Deliverance" as well as "Lord Protector." This Great One is perhaps the most well-known angel among Earth's people for he is recognized in many traditions. He is credited with seeding our planet with legions of angelics in the early Golden Age. His presence is perceived as immense, golden, and heroic and many people turn to him in their moments of need.

Historically, Michael is known as the Creator of our known Universe. He has long been associated with bearing a Sword of Light and Truth. It is said that he has given each of us a harmonic of that sword. He is noted for having long ago led the Fallen Ones back to consciousness. In the Great War of the Heavens, Michael struggled against Lucifer in the Battle between the Dark Forces and the Forces of the Light.

Michael is the Archangel who brought the first volunteers to Earth at Earth's beginning. He has vowed to serve Earth until all are fully ascended. His capacity is magnificent. One of his "jobs" is to clean out the psychic realms. He can be pictured as a knight in shining cobalt blue light healing Earth's atmosphere with his great sword. When there is any fear, call on Michael. He will also escort lost souls to the Light. His legions of Blue Ray Angels can be posted where needed.

Michael's Divine Complement is Faith. Long forgotten as a Cosmic Being, our cellular memory remembers Faith as part of the trio of Faith, Hope, and Charity. Through many patriarchal civilizations, these beings have come to be known only as the virtues that they radiate. The truth is these are the names of three of the feminine archangels who share their great service work with the better-known male archangels. As Love and Power come into balance and we move out of patriarchy and into oneness, we will reflect the Divine Polarities of God—The Divine Masculine Principle of Power as well as the Divine Feminine Principle of Love. That reflection will permeate our knowledge and become our wisdom. Call upon these archangels together or separately. They work in unison protecting and advancing faith in humans. Under both of their command are legions of Blue Ray Angels who can be posted where needed.

Invocation to Archangels Michael & Faith

I call forth Archangels Michael & Faith, of the Blue Ray of Faith, Protection, and Divine Will. I ask You to bring forth a Golden Dome of Protection. I call you now into my energy field. I ask you to wrap the cobalt blue ray of light around me and protect me. I ask that this space be surrounded by your legions of Angels of the Blue Flame. Please cut the cords of negativity with the Sword of Blue Flame. Please inspire the faith within me to grow so that I stand strong in my faith. Please align my will with the Divine Will. I thank you for being with the Earth for as long as you have been, ushering souls into higher and higher consciousness. I thank you for your dedication to the Earth and for your dedication to me. I thank you for answering my call. Help me to have faith in myself and in God. Thank you. Amen

Archangel Jophiel & Archangel Constance (also known as Christine)

Second Ray - Yellow/Gold Ray
Love/Wisdom, Constancy of Illumination, Enlightenment,
Spiritual Education, Inner Perceptions

Archangel Jophiel teaches the Power of Divine Light within each one of us. He awakens feelings for spiritual fulfillment in humankind by carrying to it the remembrance of God qualities. He also is credited with training angels to draw radiation. Together with Constance, these mighty Archangels represent constancy of light. When help is needed for meditating upon the Light, call Jophiel or Constance. In this context, light is not only the Light that can be seen on the inner planes, it stands also for "information" and greater, more expanded perceptions and wisdoms. They carry the essence of illumination which is true wisdom. They transit the quality of perpetual determination and application of wisdom. They foster spiritual education to the masses as the power of this ray ushers in awakening and ignites a longing for spiritual activity in the light. Call upon these Masters of Love and Wisdom and magnetize their virtues to you so that you may radiate them forth to others.

Invocation to Archangels Jophiel & Constance

I invoke the presence of Archangels Jophiel and Constance, You who are the Archangels of Illumination, Love/Wisdom, and Higher Perceptions. I call forth Jophiel on the Golden/Yellow Ray to expand my understanding of life, God, and self. Reveal the direction that I need to see at this time. I ask for the illumination within me so that I may see the light and bathe in the Light of God. To Constance, I ask for the translation of that Light to come forth as Wisdom now. I thank you for your Presence and for your love. Please work with me, inspiring greater and greater perceptions of Light, shining light on my path, and helping me to achieve the wisdom of the master within me. Assist me in becoming one who is constant in focus on the Light. Thank you. Amen

Archangel Chamuel &
Archangel Charity

Third Ray – Pink
Divine Love, Charity, Gratitude, Adoration,
Active Intelligence

Archangels Chamuel and Charity are the Archangels of Healing Through Divine Love. These Beloved Ones and their legions of Angels of the Pink Ray can be invoked when there is a need for the vibration and transformative energy of deep love and gratitude. Archangel Chamuel's vibration is overwhelming sweetness mixed with the strong current of caring and gratefulness. Charity's name depicts the benevolence that she embodies.

These ones are good choices for invocation when you wish to be in thanksgivingness, and when it is your desire to feel gratitude and awareness of the many blessings that are constantly bestowed upon you. The energy of this ray sparks application into a creative, active intelligence that accomplishes and organizes in our dimension. It carries the Power of Manifestation fostered by mental illumination. With just a call to Chamuel and Charity, the quality of adoring love and gracious acceptance will be showered upon the caller. As overlighting presences, you can call them directly into your heart and prepare to feel the warmth of their embrace.

Invocation to Archangels Chamuel & Charity

I call forth Archangel Chamuel and I ask that you resonate your quality of Divine Love around me now so that by resonance with your power and your glory I can come into the presence and the feeling of Divine Love. I ask that the Pink Ray Angels surround me now and remain with me during this time. I ask to be in gratitude for all the gifts that have been bestowed upon me in this life and in all lifetimes. I ask to go forward imbued with your quality—Divine Love. To live with a joyous heart. A heart that is full. I ask to work with you each day on improving these qualities within me.

Charity, help me to adore our Creator and to be a gracious servant of the Light. Bring transformative love into my heart like a sea breeze, like the sun's glistening rays that I may be renewed and inspired to act according to the vibration of the True Heart which knows only pure love. Amen

Archangel Gabriel & Archangel Hope

Fourth Ray – Crystal/White
Hope, Resurrection, Harmony

Archangels Gabriel and Hope serve mankind by helping restore latent memories and powers. They hold a Divine Concept for each individual and his/her divine plan, as well as the Divine Plan for Earth. They stimulate feelings to the outer consciousness of humankind in the hope of awakening each one's Christ Self. He assists us in raising our consciousness back to Higher awareness and helps resurrect our spiritual gifts. Calling on Gabriel assists us in reacquainting ourselves with who we truly are. They can be called upon when our intention is to restore our Selves, renew our Selves, and resurrect our Selves into the Divine Blueprint of our higher identities as Divine Humans.

In this time of radiance—as a 2,000-year cycle for Earth ends, and a new cycle begins marking the New Age of Consciousness, we call upon Gabriel and Hope to assist us in regaining our power and glory and release old patterns that no longer serve us.

Often Gabriel is associated with heralding in a new day by blowing his trumpet of light. When we find ourselves in need of help in body, mind, or spirit, we can ask him to blow his mighty trumpet where it is needed. These archangels hold the Resurrection Flame and restore Hope to the aspiring Master. She can be envisioned as the supreme goddess of the New Dawn. Call upon these Great Ones when hope and renewal are needed to harmonize your life's expression.

Invocation to Archangels Gabriel & Hope

Archangel Gabriel, I call forth and invoke your presence and the powers of love that you bring. I ask that you bring the Resurrection Flame to me that I might be resurrected, restored, and reconnected to the memories, insights, and abilities that are in my genetic blueprint. I ask to once again know the love, wisdom, and power I knew as a being of Light who chose to come to Earth. I ask that these gifts be returned to me through the power of the Resurrection Flame.

Archangel Gabriel, please resurrect the dormant Light in me so that I may be raised into the next level of vibration and understanding. Archangel Hope, please give me the endurance, and enthusiasm to realize my greatest Hope and be linked once more with the pure heart that was mine before limitation and density. Please surround me now with your presence, your love, *and with your power. I open to receive the gifts that you bring and I ask that you remain with me at this momentous time on Earth as Earth Herself is raised and restored to deeper levels of beauty, consciousness, and knowingness. Thank you. Amen*

Archangel Raphael & Archangel Mary

Fifth Ray – Emerald Green
Healing, Consecration, Concentration, Concrete Science

Archangel Raphael is "The Shining One Who Heals" and is the purveyor of remedies for physical and emotional healing. It is through Raphael that we seek guidance for overcoming dis-ease and dis-comfort. We can also call upon Raphael to help heal any separation that we feel.

Raphael teaches us dedication to humanity. Part of his work is to heal and empower the healer within us. He does this by enfolding us with the Emerald Ray. When healing is required, call upon Raphael and the Emerald Ray angels to assist and bring in the healing energies needed. Remember that Free Will will always be honored and no one can be healed without their consent. Mother Mary is Raphael's Twin Flame and is herself an Archangel. With Raphael she resonates the qualities of healing and concentration. Mary's gifts as Mother to our World are many. One of her richest offerings is focused intent; another is the healing from separation and isolation. Mary nurtures as a Divine Mother embodiment; her wings enfold the Earth and beyond.

By concentrating on service and love of God, our lives become sacred and our love is purified. Deep concentration on spiritual love brings us into resonance with the attributes of Raphael and Mary.

Invocation to Archangels Raphael & Mary

Archangels Raphael and Mary, I call forth
your great powers of healing now and the
presence of the Emerald Ray. Within this
presence and within this concentration of healing,
I ask that all levels of my being be healed,
purified, and consecrated as a Temple of Ascension and as a Temple of God. I ask you to please
bring forth the Emerald Ray Angels of Healing to
balance and align my energy.

I ask you to please bring forth the Emerald
Ray Angels of Healing to balance and align all of
my energy bodies—physical, emotional, etheric,
mental, and spiritual. Open, balance and align
my lightbody centers. Energize and align my
chakras, reconnecting and anchoring the higher
ones into my physical body. Align my earth
chakras with the body of the Earth. Raphael, help
me to reverse the aging process and begin
youthing, instead of aging. I ask that revitaliza-

tion, energy, and radiant health be imbued
within me so that I am restored to health in order
to heal others.

Mary, help me to live this life with a compassionate heart focused on the Heart of God so
that I may see the sacredness of the Eternal
mirrored everywhere. Please resonate the quality
of deep concentration, that I may learn to hold
my focus and center in the world. Help me to
understand that I am also an immaculate
concept, created in the image of God and help me
to hold in my awareness the concept of that
image until my consciousness bridges Heaven
and Earth. Thank you. Amen

Archangel Uriel &
Archangel Aurora Grace

Sixth Ray – Ruby Red
Ministration, Grace, Peace, Idealism, Devotion.

Archangel Uriel, the Dove of God, is the Archangel in charge of Guardian Angels, those angels assigned to us every lifetime who listen constantly to the prayers of our heart. Uriel ministers to all life on Earth and is often depicted as a Dove of Peace. He is remembered as the Angel who showed Enoch the celestial phenomena as well as the Angel who wrestled with Jacob in an effort to purify Jacob's conscience.

The Ruby Red Ray has been prevalent in the last 2,000 year span of human history. Its emanation gave rise to the Christian influence in much of the world through the Master Jesus. Uriel's Twin Flame is Aurora Grace. She ministers the virtues of Grace and Mercy to human embodiments as well as to the angelic line of evolution. These archangels can be invoked for the simple overlighting feeling of peace. They inspire the sweetness of devotion and minister to us in order to help each of us turn and minister to our brothers and sisters. Together these great beings resonate the qualities of reverence, purity, quietude, and idealism.

Invocation to Archangels Uriel & Aurora Grace

I call to Archangel Uriel, You who are the Dove of Peace. You who bring forth the legions of Guardian Angels who minister to each one of us as we live our lives on Earth. I call to Aurora Grace for peace in mind and in body. I ask that my prayers be heard and answered, and that I feel the response and grace of your beautiful presence. I ask for the healing that comes with Your Ruby Ray and the gift of ministering to others with Love. Help me embrace the common unity of brotherhood, sisterhood and the Oneness of which we are all a part. I ask for your great love and presence in my life. Help me to see God in others and to minister to them as family. I invoke your qualities to make the ideal real in my experience. Help me to know the devotional heart and reverence for all. Amen

Archangel Zadkiel &
Archangel Amethyst

Seventh Ray —Violet
Ascension, Invocation, Freedom, Purification,
Transformation, Transmutation, Ceremonial Magic

Archangels Zadkiel and Amethyst are called upon to consciously raise our energy and the energy in the world around us. In these times of powerful and unprecedented changes, it is the higher vibrations of the Violet Flame of Transmutation and Forgiveness that assists us in our ultimate rapture. It is to Zadkiel we turn for the purification and transformation process that will facilitate our move into the higher dimensions. The Cosmic Lady Amethyst is the essence of the Violet Ray; she brings transfiguration.

In calling upon the Violet Flame, we pull down the energy needed to change our fears into love, our doubts into true knowing, and our bodies into alignment with the new frequencies. We draw energy into our old thoughtforms and limitations to transmute ourselves and the Earth into the next level of expression.

Also known as the Ceremonial Ray, the Seventh Ray will be the primary influence during the next 2,000 year cycle of human experience. It is a powerful tool for dismantling the third dimension and establishing fourth and fifth dimensional reality where true freedom and grace prevail. Together Archangels Zadkiel and Amethyst are considered the Archangels of Ascension. The force of transformation purifies and opens the path to a higher voltage of Divine Light and Transcendence.

Invocation to Archangels Zadkiel & Amethyst

Archangel Zadkiel, I call forth Your great Light – the Violet Flame that transforms all that is negative into positive; all that is fear into love. Amethyst, I call the great power of transformation and ascension that you bring forth, the Ascension Flame and the Violet Flame, into my total experience now. Transform me and prepare me for that which lies ahead. Through the Ascension Flame, help me to hold more light. Aid me in my completion of third-dimensional life as I open to embrace the higher vibrations. I ask you to swirl the Violet Flame in, through, and around me transforming and removing every electron of discordant energy held within my physical, mental, emotional, and etheric bodies and cellular memory. I call forth your presence ever increasing and self-sustaining. I open my heart to receive the influence of the Seventh Ray deeply into myself at this time.

I call forth the Ascension energies into my consciousness to raise the frequency of my vibration for the purpose of ascending my physical body into the Light. I ask that I be raised into Light, cell by cell, molecule by molecule, atom by atom so that I, in turn, may help lift the Earth, my home, into perfect harmony. Amen

Invocation to the Archangels As a Group

Archangels and the Angelic Host, uplift me with your expanded Light and Love. I am ready to receive your guidance and radiance on the multi-dimensional levels of my being so that I may expand my dedication as a Light Worker and increase the Light that I hold, working for the good of humankind and for the good of Planet Earth.

Archangel Michael and Faith, protect me and increase my faith. Help me align my will with the Divine Will. Help me bring the energy of all that I am and all that I have ever been into true attunement with Source.

Archangel Jophiel and Constance (Christine), illuminate me with wisdom and light and help me to meditate upon the Light. Help me to see and be the Light that I am and radiate this light to others.

Archangel Chamuel and Charity, resonate divine love and gratitude to me so that by the

Law of Resonance, I may experience the fullness of divine love and then administer truth, love and light to others. Help me to forgive myself and others in order to dissolve Karma and evolve Love.

Archangel Gabriel and Hope, assist me in the resurrection of my emotional, mental, etheric, and physical bodies and personality self into my Higher or Christed Self. Grant me the eternal hope necessary to sustain and maintain myself during this time of transformation and acceleration.

Archangel Raphael and Mary, heal and align my physical, mental, emotional, and etheric bodies and help me to be a vehicle for healing others. Assist me in developing concentration. Help me dedicate myself to the path of ascension for earth and self.

Archangel Uriel and Aurora Grace, bring peace to my body, feelings, and mind so that I can live in a state of Grace and be a signpost of peace to others.

Archangel Zadkiel and Amethyst, help me transmute fear into love and assist me in calling for that which I need for my re-emergence into Higher Consciousness. Amen

—4—

Four Cosmic Beings

The book of invocations would not be complete without including within the pages an honoring of the influence and magnitude of Divine Beings who serve the many mansions of God in cosmic capacity. Far too numerous to name, for our purposes here, I have selected but four who render services and creative activity of Cosmic import. In this time of Great Radiance as we move into the Shift of the Ages, Cosmic Beings of this great proportion are now interacting with humankind. It is almost inconceivable to note that these beings who ensoul whole universes, stand on either side of the Godhead, abide at the Throne of Grace, and electrify the vibrations that affect all of Creation can be reached on a direct line. The mercy and compassion of Mother/Father God for Their Children is unfathomable for our minds. Fortunately, we can experience aspects of this kindness. We can see it in action when we consider that we can invoke the loving presence and power of Cosmic Beings and receive direct radiance, and attention from them. Truthfully we are beginning to see how we are interconnected in Oneness—all parts of the Great Wholeness, the Holiness.

With this understanding I have included invocations to The Divine Mother, Lord Melchizedek, the Mahatma, and Lord Metatron .

The Divine Mother

At the pinnacle of Differentiated Source there is one who is known as The Divine Mother. She is the full embodiment of the Divine Feminine Principle of God which is Divine Love. She serves The Oneness in concert with Divine Father, who embodies the Divine Masculine Principle of God which is Divine Power. Together these Great Cosmic Beings radiate and reflect the Balance and Perfection of the two aspects of Deity— Love and Power/Will. The Archangels, Elohim (Creator Gods and Goddesses) and Masters support this divine polarity and at each level of Creation, birth the principles into form and into all living beings.

It is said that we are created in the image of God. Divine Mother, as the Eternal Goddess or Eternal Mother of All Mothers, sustains this image from the Very Heart of God into each divine spark in every dimension. In truth, we are each a microcosm of God the Father and God the Mother—the balanced perfection of Infinite Love and Power. The Christ which completes the trinity is the Divine Child living within the Christ Self of all God-evolving beings. The angels, or messengers of the feeling nature of Source, complete the picture for they link the lower worlds with the higher realms, weaving the energies of Divine Mother into the heart, stepped-down through the dimensions of creation.

Call upon The Mother and feel the all-encompassing embrace of her nurturing heart. Let the heart describe The Mother, for no words can adequately pay tribute to this enormous fountain of flowing divine love and grace.

Slip chosen words into an invocation that the angels will convey on wings of light not confined to time or dimension and allow the heart to open to receive the Mother. Divine Mother and the lady masters have been misrepresented and forgotten on Earth as we have lived under patriarchal rule for a very long time. Little is known about the feminine forces of deity. Divine Mother IS the Holy Spirit energy. The time is ripe for the Return of the Mother, as we embrace the Paradise Vibration and come to see that we are divine sparks of a Creator with balanced male and female energy.

Invocation to Divine Mother

*I call forth a blessing and activation of
Divine Love from The Divine Mother. Mother, I
call you to enter my heart and re-birth the
Paradise Vibration in perfect balance of loving
power and the power of love.*

*I call forth all sacred light encodements and
light envelopes from your exalted heart to anchor
Love Divine into my own. Empty your heart
containing the Clear Light of God into my heart
and join with me, heart to heart, in the embrace
that I long for.*

*Let me feel myself a river with the Ocean of
Love pouring into me so that I may fill the hearts
of my brethren with the ecstasy of the Mother.*

*I call forth a Baptism of the Holy Spirit. I
call for your open heart energies to heal my
illusions of separation. I open to receive your
Eternal Love and Light so I can love god/goddess
within me and feel the rapturous union of
masculine and feminine in balance within me.*

Let this unity with You raise my Love Quotient and help me to see with the Eyes of the Heart and love from the lens of the Christ.

Beloved Mother, let me be a cosmic walk-in for your presence upon the Earth, gathering all life unto me as the beloved. Thank you. Amen

Lord Melchizedek

There is a Cosmic Being by the name of Melchizedek who presides over our entire universe. He works in a trinitized manner with Metatron and The Mahatma, the Avatar of Synthesis. He also works in concert with Archangel Michael/Faith bringing the Living Light of God through the education, resurrection and enlightenment of higher consciousness to all worlds.

The Order of Melchizedek is his universal cosmic order and the name alone may reawaken cellular memory of the tradition of spiritual wisdom associated with the many lesser orders that fit under this Great Order. Many of the Children of Light have been priests and priestesses of this tradition in other worlds and on ancient, more advanced civilizations of Earth. As we move forward in the ascension initiations, we again are reinstated within the Order and called "Melchizedeks." Melchizedek is another word for "King" and there have been various Earth masters who bore this name. Melchizedeks are divine agents of change whose heart and activities are linked to assisting the Divine Plan and purpose of the Infinite One.

Invocation to
Lord Melchizedek

Beloved Grand Master Melchizedek, I call you forth into my life as a guiding force of God current. I ask for alignment with your thought-form of Sacred Wisdom. I ask to merge with your resplendent Light Body so that I may reflect the splendor of Universal benevolence and enlightenment. I ask to bathe in your Spacious Heart and in the refined frequencies that bear your hallowed signature.

Melchizedek, transport me up to the Thrones by your mercy and open my God Eyes so I may glimpse a reflection of my Origin.

Help me drink in the image and lock the vision into the Present Now.

Help me to travel the pathways of memory, tracing my Divine Heritage, owning my Power, sensing my Glory, deciphering my distant past and Glorified future.

As I call my Spirit back into Me from all incarnations, Let me come as I Am into the fullness of Who I am and walk the Earth.

Melchizedek, please fill me with your blessings and encodements of light. Activate my chakra system and higher bodies with the touch of your Rod of Power. Help me to be a true Melchizedek Initiate—reflecting love, wisdom, and power of the One Most High in my thoughts, emotions, feelings and actions. Help the Ideal become Real for me. Thank you. Amen

The Mahatma

A gift of the Harmonic Convergence, in 1988, was the introduction to Earthlings of the energy of another Great Cosmic Being called The Mahatma. The Mahatma is a group entity who pervades all levels of consciousness and spans all dimensions up to the Source level. The Avatar of Synthesis is another name for this Immense Being of cosmic proportion. This one synthesizes all the parts of the Whole - planetary, solar, galactic, universal and multi-universal, and while the mind finds it difficult to comprehend the enormity of this Being, fortunately the heart can feel the energy and love at this level of divinity.

In fact, it is within the wish of this massive Group Being to be brought down to Earth into our awareness and experience. Quite simply we are part of this one as This Embrace spans the dimensions of reality.

Call upon this Master of Masters and experience the powerful surge of empowered love energy now gifted to humankind, as the Above and the Below become synthesized and brought into Oneness.

Invocation to
The Mahatma

I call forth to the Mahatma and ask for the greatest infusion of Mahatma energy that I can integrate at this moment in time. I ask to be flooded with this divine energy and to anchor it as a cosmic walk-in. Let me be instrumental in bringing infusions of this level of Love and Light to the planet through my body vehicle.

I call forth for an activation of my Divine Monadic Blueprint Body. Please help me to step into my deepest potentiality to carry light and love first into my Self and then into Earth. Assist me in the completion of my planetary ascension and prepare me for cosmic ascension.

O Avatar of Synthesis, let the flow of your power of ultimate union merge with my essence. I want to merge my heart into the heart of God. I want to claim that interlocking sense of the divine in all. I long to see the face of God in all faces, to hear the voice of God in all sound, and to recognize before me the countless mirrored reflections of the One teaching me wisdom and love through the Many.

Help me to transcend the lower Self. To commit to Christ Awareness. To let go of everything that binds me to limitation. To call forth the full power of my Spirit to descend into this body. To let go of everything that no longer serves my highest potential. To embody completely the I Am that I Am. To allow the nonphysical world to become more real to me than the physical.

Help me to command my Spirit 100% into the hands of God. And achieve the Oneness that I now invoke. Thank you. Amen

Lord Metatron

Representative of Source
Creator of the Electron/King of all Angels

Archangel Metatron is called "The Face of God" and "He who stands at the throne of God." He was the garment of El Shaddai in the Old Testament and Enoch's guide. He is considered the Creator of Form according to the Will of God, as well as the "Creator of the Outer Light." This most powerful Archangel is responsible for purification with Light. It is said that he controls the center of the electron. His massive service involves the re-education and rescue of worlds. And, he is heralded as the King of the Archangels.

Call upon him to repattern your energies and bring forth the New Light Encodements of New Earth/New Human. He is called upon to restructure the DNA, unlock genetic codes and co-create a new species of Light.

In this time of quickening and mutation as we move into the New Millennium, it is powerful to invoke the assistance of Metatron to raise your quotient of Light and anchor higher energetic patterns, sacred geometries, and light activations into your consciousness and into your bodies of Light.

Invocation to Metatron

I call forth Metatron and the great Fiery Ray upon which his power travels. He who repatterns the codings of light for our bodies and brings the shift into the New—the shift into the New Next dimension for self and Earth. I call forth Metatron and the influence of this great one to be present here with me, repatterning my energy fields, my DNA, and my body grid systems. I ask for whatever can be accomplished in this body, at this time, that would increase my ability to hold more light and to come fully into the highest awareness possible for me now.

Archangel Metatron, please work your wonders with me. Metatron, I ask for help in the re-chemicalization of this body, in the spiritual-ization of my blood chemistry. I ask for help in taking this temple of flesh into the Light. What-ever alchemy changes matter into light, please resonate your great Beingness here and assist me in the transmutation of the flesh itself, of the cells themselves, of all that I am into all that I can be.

Help me to anchor the Blueprint of the Perfected Etheric Body. To travel the pathways of Light Divine so I can be of greater service to humanity, the Masters, the Divine Plan of evolution, and God. I ask that you anchor your Microtron into my consciousness and into my 12-body system, supplying me with a touch of your Impulse into my electronic presence. Thank you. Amen

-5-

The Inner Plane Ascended Masters — Five Masters —

*H*uman beings who have incarnated within physical experience sufficiently to evolve their mastery of energy, light, and consciousness to the degree that they have attained freedom from rounds of reincarnation are called inner plane Ascended Masters. They are, by definition, free of karma and have passed through the various mastery levels—or initiations—to consciously ascend into the Light. Inherent in this understanding is that they achieved mastery in controlling what is called the four-body system or, the *mental body*, the *emotional body*, the *etheric body*, and the *physical body*. Although many ascensions were made after death of the body, some were achieved by raising the body into light while still present in it. They have overcome the limitations of the third dimension and moved into higher dimensions by means of raising the vibratory rate of their bodies to a higher frequency enabling an accelerated state of beingness. They embody Christ Consciousness which enables absolute and limitless Love, Divine healing, precipitation, materialization, dematerialization and many more powerful gifts. To those with more limited awareness, these acts appear to be "miracles."

As the Ascended Masters for Earth serve God in Creation, they dedicate themselves to Earth and humanity for a given length of time. They assist us and are open to our calls for they work to bring God consciousness to us. Eventually, they themselves ascend from this level of operation and serve in yet higher capacities. It is said that they can only move on in their own evolution when others have sufficient light to take their places. In a sense, we are all ascended masters in training to fill their shoes, thus allowing them to move on to a more universal influence.

Ascended Masters make their presence known to us through the deeper levels of our own intuition. Their wisdom and guidance can come to us by opening up to higher dimensions through the practice of meditation and prayer. Their influence is felt telepathically and may result in any number of manifestations such as *channeling*, perceiving their forms physically, or simply hearing their words on the inner planes. The help of an inner place Ascended Master is incomparable because their understanding is based on the experience of Earthly lives. As prototypes for our future selves, they are excellent focuses for Invocations.

It is said that there are 144,000 Ascended Masters in the Office of Christ within the Spiritual Hierarchy of

Earth. Many are known by familiar names; more often their names are not known. They are associated with every religious tradition on Earth and each one carries the vibration of Christ Consciousness and is therefore a "Christ." Master Jesus, whose ascended name is Sananda, probably ranks among the best known of these beings of light. Gautama-Buddha, the fully enlightened manifestation of Wisdom, Truth, and Love is another Ascended Master. Lord Buddha holds the position of Planetary Logos for Earth.

Mother Mary has made herself available as teacher and comforter on the Earth Plane for 2,000 years. Other well-known Ascended Masters are Saint Germain, Krishna, Djwhal Khul, Serapis Bey, Kuthumi, Confucius, El Morya, Kwan-Yin and many, many others. These beings are incredible sources of loving guidance and readily attend to our requests within Divine Order and Timing.

The inner place Ascended Masters are extensions of God—just as we are—but their function within Creation has become substantially elevated over many lifetimes of noble accomplishments. They are our older brothers and sisters looking after us in our Earthly journey and are considered role models for our future selves. Invoking the presence of an Ascended Master brings the opportunity to gain deeper understanding and clarity with regard to our individual goals and potential.

Many of us worked side by side with them before choosing to come to Earth. Many of us will return to work with them in the Brotherhoods and Sisterhoods of

Light. Many of us ask their assistance to help spark our memories of those occasions before we descended into matter for the experiment and experience of descending light into matter and then ascending matter back into light. The very act of being born into a third dimensional body denotes—in most cases—a forgetfulness of times before. It is important to remember that our own divine I Am Presence contains all the love and wisdom of the Masters and that deep within our True Self we are indeed masters disguised as humans evolving. If we can keep the bigger picture in mind, we will avoid mystification and worship. The Ascended Masters do not want us to be in awe of them. They are merely mirrored reflections of our highest selves. They want us to attain Christ Consciousness within our present incarnation and co-create Heaven on Earth. Then Earth can ascend into the higher dimensions and take her rightful place in the Heavens.

For clarity's sake, it is important to add here that there are Ascended Masters living on the Earth presently. In prior times initiates left their bodies behind when they passed through the higher levels of spiritual initiation or advancement. Now it is possible to complete high level initiations and retain the physical vehicle. As we move into the next Golden Age we will indeed see a Christ Race living in embodiment on Earth. Therefore many high level initiates on the planet are now passing into the beginning stages of ascension and can be called "Ascended Masters" within a certain perspective.

Invocation to the Inner Plane Ascended Masters

Ascended Masters, I open to your guidance, love, and assistance in my spiritual growth on all levels of my being. When I am awake, communicate and radiate your wisdom and insight to me so that, by resonance with your divine energies, I may raise my lower self into the higher consciousness. When I sleep, instruct me on the inner levels. Help me to fulfill my destiny to remember the fullness of my potential so that I may step into my full physical and spiritual presence upon the Earth. Show me how to take my rightful place in the evolution now taking place on the Earth. Thank you all for your diligent teachings and sacred companionship. Amen

Lord Sananda

Lord Sananda is the Higher Self, Higher Dimensional Vibration of the Ascended Master who lived one of his incarnations as Jesus the Christ. Sananda, long considered the "Son" of God has the service of bringing "sonship" and "daughtership" to us so we can know the victory and attainment of Creation as Whole Light Beings, as "Christs" merged with our Divinity. He is considered World Teacher along with Kuthumi.

Two thousand years ago his mission was to seed Christ Consciousness on the planet. To mirror to humanity what was possible to be achieved by human consciousness. In the crucifixion he reenacted the death of the lower self, the ending of limitation and hate, the uprooting of old patterns and thoughtforms, victory over the flesh, and the transcendence of the physical body into the Christed Body of Light. In the resurrection, he demonstrated the lifting of consciousness back into its grander dimensions. He exemplified power over death. He planted the seed for restoration and renewal of love and light and the reconnection to Self and God. He demonstrated that we must die to our lower consciousness and be resurrected into our Radiant Selves. Sananda demonstrated the victory of compassion and how compassion and the higher emotions literally affect our DNA and unlock the genetic codes for resurrecting the Christ. By embodying forgiveness, he demonstrated transcendence of the lower nature. He then offered humanity a template for their physical ascension into the light, as he made his own ascension in public. As Jesus, he served as a Master with humility as he washed his disciples' feet.

As Sananda, he is still active in helping humanity realize Christ potential. His love is just a heartbeat away for he is dedicated to the establishment of a Christ Race upon the Earth. Know that you may ask him to touch your heart and open it. (He will give you the Archetype of the Christ.)

Call upon Sananda, The Heart Master, when you want to feel the Christed Heart and Love. As a demonstration of Resurrection and Ascension, he is available to assist ascending masters. His love is extremely deep and profound.

At planetary and cosmic levels this being, often referred to as The Most Radiant One, always brings forth the simple yet divine revelation that the Kingdom of God is "Within" us and "Without." According to Sananda, knowing oneself to be a Son or Daughter of God is a prerequisite for true healing, which is healing the grand illusion of separation.

Call upon Sananda and feel the majesty and magnitude of his presence and sweet love. His energy is much more extensive and powerful than the energy of any of his embodiments alone. His original spiritual "Creation" at Source was before Creation, when he came forth as a Kumara being—from a field of energy that was before Creation.

Invocation to Sananda

(I)

Gracious One, draw me into the radiation, the current of energy that is your Expanded Heart. Help me to follow in your compassionate footsteps. To raise my self into The Christ that I AM and to shine forth majestically from that hallowed position through eternity. Lift me into your Heart, my Heart, and the Heart of All God.

Bless me with patience mixed with determination, gentleness with strength, inner experience of Light with outer activity of the Light, so that I may become Whole—a lifestream reflecting the Heart of a child and the Mastery of the Masters, Heaven and Earth, and All That Has Ever Been. Thank you. Amen

Invocation to Sananda
(II)

*Before Father/Mother God I come as a Child
Christ, an unfolding spectrum of Christ Consciousness bursting forth into completion. And as
I step forward with intention for self-mastery I
call upon my heart which holds the indwelling
Inner Christ. I call upon Sananda, the Heart
Master who brings the power of love sufficient to
open the heart to the fields of pure love and light
that lie* IN POTENTIA *within me.*

*Oh, Sananda, even as I speak your name the
comfort comes like a blanket wrapped about this
Child that I am. O, Sananda, even as your name
joins with the air around me, the call is answered. For in your name is held the vibration of
all that a soul here longs for. For in your name
lies an essence of power, love, wisdom, and
sweetness of the Christ. You project the longing in
my True Heart. The vibration of your love and
service to the Earth quickens me, prepares me,*

and overlights the path to Christ Consciousness. I call you close to me, as close as you can come within the parameters of my highest good, within the boundaries of Divine Will and the Divine Plan for me.

Come into my heart and resonate True Compassion to the fields of light that comprise my beingness here on Earth. Lift me, teach me, overlight me, and strengthen me. Help me to reach the love principle that somehow I know is possible. I know it as a distant memory. I know it as a bell ringing in the distance. I know it as the whisper of my Beloved, as a feeling not felt for a long time. Be in the wind, in the air, in the flower's scent, in the midnight hour of silence, in the glistening that accompanies the night shawl that wraps itself about me.

O, Sananda, walk with me. The Christ with the Ascending Christ. Enfold me in your radiation that I might take one more anointed step in my Divine Heritage, the perfume of Home. Amen

Mother Mary

Mother Mary, the Archangel, the Mother of Jesus, the Compassionate Divine Mother lights the Earth and is a light in all the Heavens. She directs legions of angels and is a representative of Divine Grace to humankind. She is considered to be the Cosmic Mother to un-ascended humankind and is a great stabilizing power of protection. Motherhood is a service to Master Mary; it is said that she assists with the hearts of incoming children prior to birth. With Archangel Raphael, she also serves in a healing capacity. Her presence can be felt just by the simple calling of the heart. Ask for the healing touch of her love. Ask for the vibration of the Waters of Life that she carries to flow into your beingness. They will re-awaken the remembrance of the divine connection that is within soul memory. Ask for the loving power of perseverance to help you as you attain to heights within yourself.

As mother of Jesus, Mary held the Immaculate Concept of her son becoming the Christ. She held the image of that perfection for him during his entire pres-ence on Earth. She is the personification of perseverance and concentration. Mary embodies the Mother Prin-ciple of God: healing, nurturing, accepting divine love and patience. Her color is the sky blue that evokes the Feeling of peace. Call upon her for help in sustaining these virtues within you.

Invocation to Mary

Minister unto me, O healing One of Pure Love, that I might find my eternal way back into wholeness, balance and harmony. Let the Waters of Life that you carry wash over me cleansing and clearing my road to our Father/Mother God. Help me to hold an Immaculate Concept of myself as a Risen One, in my higher ascended body holding enough light and love to vibrate out of third and fourth dimensions into the higher dimensions of deep love awaiting me.

Help me to forgive and move on, step by step, into the brightness of this Transformative Hour. When I need a mother, let my head rest upon your gown of light. Help me to feel and recall pure acceptance and the light of passionate encouragement. Overlight me with the feminine aspect of Total Love that you embody. Thank you. Amen

Saint Germain

Presiding over the Seventh Ray, Beloved St. Germain can be called the Director for the present 2000-year cycle, or the *New Age*. He represents Freedom to the Earth. With the Violet Transmuting Flame of Forgiveness, his service is transmuting the old patterns of the past and replacing them with the template of perfection.

Through many incarnations, St. Germain has involved himself with humankind's freedom. More than any other Ascended Master, he has worked mostly with the humans and physical life. Some of his more famous incarnations were as the Prophet Samuel, Joseph, father of Jesus, and Merlin in the court of King Arthur. He lived as Roger Bacon, father of science, and Christopher Columbus. His last embodiment was as Francis Bacon, the English writer and philosopher who wrote many of the Shakespearean plays. He even lived on Earth in his ascended form for the purpose of raising the consciousness of civilizations, calling himself St. Germain, meaning "Holy Brother." He lived with continuity of consciousness as he remembered each embodiment.

As an Ascended Master he brought the I Am instruction to the world in the 1930s. He is a great force behind the Violet Flame of Transformation and Transmutation and will answer the call of humanity for help in this time of transformation.

At this time he steps forward in his evolution and embraces the position of Master or Teacher of all of the Masters of the Seven Rays of Creation. Since "chohan" is a word the ascended ones use to convey the meaning of "Head" or "Leader," he is called "Mahachohan" meaning Great Teacher.

Lady Portia, Goddess of Justice, is the Lady Master who is his Divine Complement and who serves by his side. She serves on the inner planes on what is called the Karmic Board. Feel encouraged to call on her help when justice needs to prevail.

Invocation to St. Germain

I invoke the presence of St. Germain, carrying the Violet Flame of transmutation and forgiveness unto the world. I call Beloved St. Germain to come as a comrade in this Time of Freedom to enable me to hold my focus on the unending, unfolding of the petals of the Freedom Flower. As each petal opens us to reveal a greater sense of freedom, transmit to me the understanding and experience of the bliss of freedom from all limitation. Inspire within me the 7th ray of invocation, transformation, sacred ceremony, magic, order and Ascension. Help me to gain control of thoughts and emotions. Help my actions to be God-directed. Help me to dedicate myself to life as you have dedicated yourself to humanity.

Resonate your power of love to drive out discord within and around me so that I can be my Self at last—a God-being expressing myself on Earth as I do in Heaven. Amen

Kwan Yin

Known as the "One who hears the cries of the world," Kwan Yin is the Goddess of Mercy and Forgiveness who cares for all of humankind. Her vibration is one of deep compassion, joy, and serenity. It is said that she embodies all that is feminine in the Universe. Having taken the Bodhisattvic Vow, when she became enlightened she chose to keep her human form instead of transcending into pure energy. She wanted everyone to attain enlightenment and has vowed to remain with the Earth in her Ascended Form until everyone on Earth is enlightened. She is called the Queen of China and she is beloved by all who feel her healing vibration. Call upon her love and mercy and she will respond with overwhelmingly gracious love.

It is said that she embodies the Divine Mother aspect of Buddhism. Call forth her presence and assistance and spend some time sitting with her energy. She is a perfect blend of love, wisdom, and power. As she serves on the Karmic Board, you may choose to call upon her for the merciful completion of karma.

Invocation to Kwan Yin

Kwan Yin, I call forth your unwavering dedication to humanity and to each human soul and heart for the peace of true healing. I ask you to now stand beside me and shower me with the rays of healing love that you carry. Your vibration is respondent with the compassionate vibration of God's love for the Children of Light. Touch me with the soft strength of your conviction, your ever-flowing Grace and Beauty, the fullness of your Heart. Pour into me and let me be the golden cup receiving the healing elixir of your beingness so that my cup can run over with health, vitality, rejuvenation, and connection to Source. Blend your current with my own to give a boost to the course of this River merging now into the Ocean of Mercy. Thank you. Amen

Kuthumi

Ascended Master Kuthumi is known for his gentle nature as he serves in the area of illumination and education. Offering his understanding and wisdom through his love, he instructs humankind that each one is made up of the divine essence called love. He directs us to seek the Master within and says that we are all each other's brother and sister.

Prior incarnations were as the Greek philosopher Pythagoras, Balthazar (one of the three Wise Men) John the Beloved, and St. Francis of Assisi. His connection is strong to all of life, including the nature and animal kingdoms.

It is said that he is next in line to Lord Maitreya, the Planetary Christ. He hold the position of Lord of the Second Ray of Love/Wisdom.

Along with Sananda, Kuthumi also serves as World Teacher. He works closely with Djwhal Khul who runs the Interdimensional Synthesis Ashram located in the second ray ashram of Kuthumi. You can invoke Kuthumi's dear presence in meditation and experience his energy first-hand.

Invocation to Kuthumi

*Beloved Kuthumi, teach me to walk the
gentle path of love and wisdom. Help me to
understand the unity of life present in all of the
kingdoms and to do my part in uniting the
elemental, human, and angelic kingdoms. I call
forth for your loving nature to blend with me and
soothe my emotional body. Resonate your light
and love to me and be my brother, so that I may
feel and reawaken the Master within me. Beloved
Kuthumi, let me see into the soul of animals.
Show me how to increase my vibration and at the
same time slow down and notice the color of the
rose. I know the world around me is vibrant and
glowing. Without my worldly concerns I can
perceive the light of the world. Walk with me as
my Brother through nature unfolding my heart
like the petals of the rose. And inspire me to look
within myself for the golden truth that lies within
the lotus heart. Thank you. Amen*

–6–

Healing the Self

*C*ountless books have been written addressing the age-old questions, "Who am I?" "What is my *Self*?" On one level, "Self" is the I Am Presence or Individualized God Presence or monad. It begins with that part of you that can say, "I Am," and continues farther into infinity than can be comprehended in normal awareness. To heal the Self is to gather-in—to draw toward our consciousness—the *greater experience* in order to merge with our vast potential and become our pure God Self. Our greatest potential lies in the Oneness that all beings move toward in their expansion. As we reach up to embrace these higher aspects of ourselves, we are invoking the I Am Presence. Coming into union with the I Am Presence and interacting within its radiance is a very powerful experience and a substantial step in personal evolution.

There is also a potential self called the "Christ Self," or "Anointed Self." To be "Christed," one presents their being for full containment of the Light. This light becomes manifest when your total intention is one of unconditional love both for yourself and all other beings. As a Christed Being, you bring comfort, healing, and compassion to all you encounter and are in union with the monad.

In order to evolve into these elevated states of consciousness, and to sustain them in every day life, all levels of our awareness must come into grace through healing. *Healing the "Self" means mending the separation between ourselves and Source.* The memories of our true nature are locked into each cell of our living bodies and each spiritual step—each effort toward true healing—is an attempt to bring these memories into consciousness. Allowing these memories to unfold through meditation, prayer, and by invoking the assistance of higher beings, awakens the traveller on the road Home where true joy awaits.

The invocations on the following pages may be performed to ask for these elevated levels of awareness. They are designed to loosen the ties to the illusion of separation. With patience, time, and devotion, you will feel the changes taking root in your life. Embracing the I Am Presence and the Christ-Self is the means toward perfect expression of self. The I Am Presence knows only perfection; the Christ Self is perfected, but has knowledge and memory of the personality self which believes in imperfection. Among other aspects of our great identities, we are a sum total of the three—a Holy Trinity. The goal would be to merge the personality,

Higher Self or soul, and I Am Presence. Merging our consciousness with the divine consciousness is a step-by-step process. But it is inherent within us—for we are ourselves aspects of The Divine.

Invocation to the I AM Presence

Beloved I AM Presence, the Eternal God Presence I AM, enfold me in your love. Place a pillar of white light around me to protect me and allow your rays of Light to anchor firmly in my heart. Instill within me your Divine qualities, so in purity and humility I can fulfill the Divine Plan set forth for me in Heaven.

Beloved I AM Presence, lift me up into my Christ Self—the bridge between my physical self and you forevermore. Embracing my Christed Self, empower me with Ascended Master Consciousness, the consciousness of Truth and Bliss.

Beloved I AM Presence, help me to accelerate the frequency of my vibration and growth and transform me into unity with you. You are the blueprint of My True Self. I invoke the resonance of your Divine Presence to assist my lesser self in coming into unity with the truth of who and what I am.

Beloved I Am Presence, anchor firmly in my heart and merge into my physical, etheric, emotional and mental bodies as I prepare to raise the light quotient. I call for this merger to be on every level of my existence and awareness. Amen

Invocation for Attaining Christ Consciousness

*I call forth to the Inner Plane Ascended
Masters and Angels and ask for assistance on all
levels for attaining Christ Consciousness. I ask to
merge with the monad or I Am Presence so that
the Presence will take dominion over my personality and cell self. I ask to think with the super-
conscious mind or Christ Mind and feel with the
higher emotions of a Christ Heart.*

*I ask for the removal of the illusion of
separation from GOD so that I may know myself
as a Daughter (Son) of GOD—a seed carrier of
God Consciousness. I seek to lift my thoughts,
feelings, words and actions to the perfected state
of a Christ. I ask for the removal of core fear and
all of its many faces. I ask for help in transmuting negative ego consciousness into Christ
consciousness.*

*I call forth to the company of Heaven to
reprogram my subconscious mind with living
patterns of affirmations written in the Language
of Light. Let sacred geometries, key and codes*

deposit the virtues of total unconditional love, forgiveness and reverence for all life into my subconscious mind.

I ask for help in walking into the new millennium with the Masters and the Angels as an externalization of the hierarchy. Let compassion unlock the genetic codes for the resurrection of my Radiant Self. Let death to the lower self be accomplished! I want to demonstrate the potential of a Christ and add my light to the Christ Consciousness grids surrounding Mother Earth. Help me to unplug from Mass Consciousness and plug fully into Christ Consciousness Now! Amen

Invocation to the Heart of Source

To Father/Mother God

*In our hearts and with as much of our soul's
light as we can gather about us, we step before
the thrones of Father/Mother God to ask for the
blessing of radiant unfoldment within the Heart
of The One.*

*We reach into our hearts and pull forth our
awakening like a tender, yet strong seedling. We
notice the colors; there is more than green there.
A veiled paintbrush has placed a rainbow of
color, like a wash, over our beingness. If we look
deeply we can see layers upon layers of color and
vibration peeking through the limbs of the
seedling of our awakening. Our glorious cosmic
past shines through in hues pieced together like a
cosmic quilt gathered in higher dimensions before
our descent into third dimensional Earth.*

*Within the mirror of the seedling we are,
there is a mighty Tree of Life containing all that
we have ever been, containing All That Is. Within
it, the story of every ascension and descension of*

Spirit into Matter, of life after life, of all the
history and dictionary of the outpourings of the
Divine Spark that We Are.

Once again, we offer up our Wholeness
within the sprouting seedling in the expression of
Sacred Union: the marriage of divine and
human, form and formless, all the heavens and
all the earths. Once again, we plant ourselves
consciously within the Heart of God and invoke
the Waters of Life - the Golden Tears of Ecstatic
Joy, of Union, and of Completion to rain down
upon us to insure steady, beautiful, and conscious
evolution within the limitless fields of the Heart
of Source, Your Heart. Amen

Invocation to the Devic Kingdom

We open to that aspect of Divine Mother known as NATURE *and invoke the divine presences of light present in millions upon millions of worlds within worlds, the Devic Kingdom. We ask to be connected to the devas that reside in the plants, trees, flowers, and rocks. We call to the intelligence and God Sparks that quietly mold the grasses and direct, with invisible paintbrushes, the rainbow palette of colors into the faces of flowers.*

We call to the overlighting Devas of the Four Elements who radiate their blessings to the human race. To the tiny intelligences that carry the breeze, dance in the firelight, caress our bodies in their waterdance, and institute the vibration of the many faces of land masses that hold our bodies. We invoke the call to the kingdoms, paying special tribute to the unity of all kingdoms. Asking to feel connected to air, water, earth, and fire and the ethers. To the devas alive within the body of Earth and within our own bodies.

We call to the devas who are the beings who empower each cell. We ask you to co-create with the Angels of greater size and let go of negativity at the cellular level. We ask the cell devas to open to the light of source, let go and be restored.

We ask to feel aliveness on all levels of life. We ask to feel connected to all expressions of creation in form. We ask to be united with all aspects of the expression of God streaming through us and circulating, undulating, and spiralling all around us.

Let the hidden secrets of Oneness be now revealed! We call from our bodies containing civilizations of consciousness to wake up to the power of life running through us. We ask that our vision and senses become aware of the dimensions of life flowing before us of which we have been unaware.

All this we invoke in this time of radiance approaching, as we ask for an invocation to Great Awareness of all life, infinite and infinitesimal, within us and within all things. Thank you. Amen

Invocation to the Inner Child

I invoke the child within me to stand up and walk to me, meeting me on the bridge of Unity. Come forward, Dear Small One, now. Come out to play. It has been far too long that I have kept you hidden, locked into confinement, unseen and unheard by myself and others.

I need you now for my completion. You know the expression of my Joy. You know how to catch moonbeams in your hands. How to bring the Earth in through your toes. How to reach to the stars without measuring distance. You know how to walk into the mountains in your heart and with your little eyes locked onto the horizon.

I call you, Sweet Part of Myself, to trust me and open your heart to me. We are part of the Same One. I recognize that you are no stranger to rejection and to separation. Together we shall set our sails on the Ocean of Oneness and Unity. Together we can be complete. Together we can heal and pick up our mantle and be Our God Parents' Happy Child.

I bless you and promise to care for you, listen to you, know you, and love you. For too long you have crouched in unlit hallways. Now bask in the Light with me. Warm yourself in the sunshine of our existence together. Let us walk hand in hand. Let us take turns in this body. Sometimes you will lead and I will follow. Sometimes I will lead and you will follow. We can co-create our days and nights in awareness of one another.

You need me to acknowledge your presence and set you free. I need you to set my course for Freedom. Together we can move into the Era of Freedom. Amen

Invocation to My Heart

I invoke the opening of my Heart.

I ask that my Higher Self descend down upon me and lift me into the Field of Heart where Love is nestled. Transport me to the Secrets of the Heart, the Expansion of the Heart, and the Wisdom that lies therein.

Let me be one who moves from the Heart and speaks from the Heart. Who listens from the Heart, and who reaches toward Heaven from the Heart.

O Heart, open to me! Teach me your ways! Hold my attention. Be my Peace. Help me to sit and dwell within you. Be the comfort zone that I require. Be the safety net for me in a world that can seem chaotic.

O Heart, flood my entire being and color my flesh with the shimmer of your glow. Flow into my body, into my hair, into my eyes, into my skin and organs. Circulate into the heart and center of each cell. This is my prayer, for my Heart is part of the Heart of God. I seek the

Inner Heart, the Heart that is real, the Heart that holds the Truth of reality.

I ask for a quiet mind so that Heart can be heard as I move through my days. I ask for your guidance as I dwell in the silence of my meditations.

Strengthen my capacity to live a Heart-centered life so my actions can be bathed in love. Teach me your ways so that I may sing my Heart Song. Amen

Invocation to the Silence

Come let me know you. Come wrap the deep petals of your Love around me and bring me into the center, into the nectar, into the heart of this most precious flower of Silence. The silent flower that bursts forth opening and opening and opening. Let me feel the one breath pouring in within this vibration.

I knock upon the door of Silence to hear not thoughts. But to hear that which occupies the space of no-thought. I knock upon the door of Silence to hear the celestial harmonies that play endlessly within the silence of the worlds within worlds. For when the world's and the mind's chatter ceases, there is such a sweet music—a symphony played by the angel within me.

I invoke the drawing of this sweet music of the spheres into the deepest parts of myself. And I invoke the Light of the vibration of life within me. Let the Light pour out of a golden chalice of 10,000 liquid suns. And when it is that I am moving through the world, help me to yet feel the

*silent sanctuary within the heart beckoning to me
to remember the honor of your presence. I invoke
the power of Silence that unites my heart with the
Heart of Creation, that Silence that binds my
breath to the Breath of the Universe.*

*I call forth the remembrance of Silence, the
experience of Silence, the connection to the
Silence, the sound of Silence, the peace of Silence,
the Presence of my Christed Brethren joining in
the Silence.*

*I ask you to sweep over me like a great wave,
bringing together the ebb and flow of the Oneness. Come now, Sweet Sister Silence. Sweet
Brother of Completion. Wash over me with the
rhythm of Creation. Bring my tears into that
great ocean and help me, dear Silence, to dissolve
my separation into Oneness. Amen*

Invocation to My Physical Body Deva

I invoke the Spirit of the Physical Body that I live in. I call upon you to open my physical body to the energies of Resurrection and Transformation. I ask that all doors to this body be open to let the energies that would transform it to a higher frequency pour forth elegantly and easily into this body now.

I ask that the energies of rejuvenation come to me now. In through the top of my head, through my eyes, through the pores of my body and into my blood. I ask that all organs, all systems in this body, open to receive great infusions of light and energies in preparation for my expanded consciousness.

I ask that this body be readied to wear a new gown, a seamless garment of light in the approaching radiance. I ask that energies of Restoration, Transmutation, Transformation, Resurrection, and Ascension descend into my body to deliver it from all excesses, from all dis-ease, from all negative patterns, ego and energy, and from all lethargy that would bog it down. Let the essence of Light itself pour through my veins, my bones and cells, quenching my thirst for renewal.

I ask that the blueprints of Ascension be handed to my Body Deva to be utilized.

Let my body eliminate that which no longer serves it; excesses of weight, excesses of burden, excesses of discordant energy. I invoke this on my authority as a Child of God. And I ask that the changes be inside and outside, subtle and apparent. Bring radiance into this body of mine. Let all manifestations of the illusion of aging be now reversed. I call to abide in a temple of radiant health and youthful perfection.

I ask for this now in the fullness of this hour, that my flesh be lifted into the Light. Amen

Invocation for a Divine Mate

I call to myself the energies that unite the Male and the Female who will stand together and not diminish each other's Light, but embrace the Divine and bring forth the highest and the best in one another.

I ask for a partner at this time who will love and accept me within the wholeness of their being, one who will accept my capacity to love unconditionally. I am ready to bring the totality of all I have been, all roles I have played, to the light of union with another. I ask for a union in joy and respect to support each other's journey back to Source. Let me find my companion in balance so that together we may anchor our light into the World.

I ask for the help of Divine Father and the help of Divine Mother to bring to me an integrated, ascended relationship of unconditional love for I am now ready. I thank all who will assist and all who have prepared me to call this forth. Amen

–7–

Healing for Others

As we begin to feel that we are one great family with the same Father/Mother God, we cannot help but begin to recognize that each one is our Brother and our Sister. It becomes our yearning to see God in one another and in ourselves. With this increased perception, we will be able to love as Christed Beings— unconditionally and completely. Loving others means healing others, for we begin to have the same wish for others as for ourselves. When we feel our oneness, we know that humanity is like one large being who needs healing. What needs to be healed? It is our feelings of separation, fear, doubt, discord, and emptiness. As Children of the Light, it is our covenant to come back to Source and rekindle that awareness in others.

Eventually we rekindle our Covenant with God to bring back God Consciousness to the Children of Light. As we awaken, we take our place among the Ascended Masters, joining them in their service to Earth or other worlds.

For a Friend
Experiencing Illness

I invoke the presence of Lord Raphael and Mary, Archangels of Healing, the hierarchy healing teams and the Emerald Ray Healing Angels, and Dr. Lorphan from the inner plane of Sirius to please be with my friend who is undergoing medical treatment at this time. I invoke the power and love of my friend's physical body deva and ask it to bring forth comfort and ease. Let the healing be immediate and complete as God would have it be. Let the process be tempered by the presence of Divine Beings.

Bring resiliency, rest, strength, and harmony into the body so the energies of rejuvenation and revitalization can come in as the healing is realized.

Guide the hands that care for my friend with wisdom and gentleness. Imbue those hands with powerful healing light. Let each participant in this experience move through the challenge with grace and serenity, allowing for the energy to move toward a positive and rewarding outcome.

Be present in my friend's awareness so he/
she will know all is well. Grant the insight to rise
above what the body may choose to experience,
and show a way to grow without pain. May all
who visit emanate great love. Let my friend bask
in the radiance of Your healing love

I ask for his/her own Guardian Angel to be
ever-attendant during this challenge. Let this
experience result in great bursts of joy as my
friend moves closer to a newer self. Let my friend
be resurrected into a new body of Light and
transformation as the process completes itself in
Love and long life. Amen

Transmutation of
AIDS

Let this be an invocation to the healing of those who hold the disease in their body called AIDS; and let this lack of ease, this enigma, this illness afflicting so many, now be held in the Light. Let the blessing of Father/Mother God come upon those who have aligned with this pattern.

Like all challenges, AIDS is a teacher. Let this teacher leave and the lesson be learned. Remove this lesson if doing so is within the Divine Plan for these souls.

If this dis-ease has been manifested by humankind's selfishness, carelessness, mistreatment of science, hatred, or confusion, let those qualities be turned to love and clarity. Let the seed which has allowed and propelled this energy into the form that it now holds, be stopped, sublimated, and ceased.

Let the reason, the cause, be now held in the Light. Let the human beings living upon the Earth no longer require this or any disease. Bring, instead, an easy awakening so that all can see dis-ease is no longer needed for transformation.

I invoke, I invoke, I invoke the release of this pattern. I ask that a dispensation of Light, Love and Healing come forth into the virus itself and to those who hold the pattern.

Archangel Raphael, if this is in accordance with the plan for Earth, permeate through that which is called AIDS and bring the Angels of Comfort to those who are fading from us with this affliction.

I invoke an easy transition for those who are departing. Let their consciousness be strong, alert and alive as the doors open into the next realm. I invoke an understanding and a forgiveness of the pain. Let the vibration of God's love be strongly felt. I invoke a forgiveness of the choices that these lifestreams chose, the patterns of rejection, the difficulties chosen in order to grow. Rush the Emerald Waters over these patterns. Let the Healing Waters of the Emerald Ray of Healing carry them past suffering. Amen

From a Parent to a Child

I invoke the presence of the Angels and the Masters who work with and assist my beloved child (name). I call forth the Higher Self of that precious one who has lived in my home and still lives in my heart. I ask Higher Self to convey my love as he/she grows and takes a place in the world of experience.

I ask for protection and care for my child (name) and ask that her Guardian Angels stand close in my stead. I invoke the opening of this child's heart and mind to that which is unseen, unheard, and not yet felt. Let the energies of Ascension and Wisdom be brought forth. Bring in the energies of great Love and Transformation, in accordance with free will.

O Child, flesh of my flesh! One who slumbered within my temple. Awaken now to your glory, your goodness, your great Universal Self!

I enfold you in my wings—your place in my heart is forever, whatever the distance between us.

I call to your Ecstatic Self and invoke the awakening and connection to Spirit that will rejoin you to the realms of Gods and Goddesses. To your true identity as a Child of God, Amen

For Healing Another

I call forth the Great Healing Waters of Life to pour through this body, these hands, these eyes and this heart. Let my consciousness and being now resonate with the Masters and Angels of Healing. Let the healing of Divine Light come through me now.

Let that which is appropriate take place in the lifting of pain, in the lifting of uncertainty, in the lifting of the abuses of the heart, and in the lifting of love's obstacles.

As we breathe and as my hands are held upon this body and this heart, let the energies of the God Force come forth now to heal and to place the signature of the Christ upon her (him). Let that which is ready to be released be released in the light of protection, in the comfort and safety of this environment, and with the Angels of Healing and Love standing by. Let the energies of transmutation and forgiveness pour through us.

I ask for my energies to be raised in order to minister light and healing. Let me be an instrument of lovingkindness now and for all time. So be it. Amen

To End Addictions

I call forth Archangel (Mother) Mary and the Angels of Healing and Compassion to lend a helping hand now as I face my addictions. I ask to be surrounded with the vibration of acceptance and non-judgment so that I can love and accept myself as I am. I am determined to actively participate in transforming myself into a confident, wholly conscious and complete being who can let go of addictive tendencies and behaviors now.

I ask for the Flame of Forgiveness to ignite within my heart so that I can forgive any who may have knowingly or unknowingly contributed to my present condition. I forgive, I forgive, I forgive. I ask for recognition of the lessons that have been orchestrated for me for my own growth and empowerment and the understanding that I no longer require the same lessons.

Help me, Mary, to turn with love to my past and let the Waters of Life wash over any lifetimes when I have carried pain, rejection, and low self-esteem. Angels, help me to heal the roots of my dis-ease. Let the core of my problems be washed and purified in the light of transformation. I am *ready to step out of the old mold of dependence and be fulfilled by the power and love of the Eternal. Help to remove any karmic patterns of addictions.*

I invoke all Beings of Light who can assist me, strengthen me, and help me to remember the fullness of who I am. I want now to be filled from within and from the Light of God that is every-where. Amen

To Clear Fear

I call forth the Masters and Angels who work with disassembling core fear within human consciousness. I call forth Master Djwhal Khul, St. Germain, Lady Portia, and Archangels Amethyst, Zadkiel and Faith.

I call forth the Violet Flame of Transformation and Forgiveness to transmute fear into love—all the way to the cellular level. I ask that fear be removed gently and with ease, but as quickly as possible, so that I can know more Love.

Let Fear be no more!

In the Sacred Fire of cleansing I ask to be given the capacity, determination, and desire to let go of old programs within my consciousness that are fear-based and to let go of fear of change. I ask for the rainbow of knowable things to arch around me and color me with the sacred information in the Language of Light that will forever set me free. From Ascended Master Djwhal Khul I call for the Core Fear Removal Program to enter my consciousness. Amen

Invocation to the Angel of the House

I invoke the Angel of the House to stand forth in purity as an example of Grace, Harmony, and Love—those qualities that I wish to be present in this dwelling. I ask you to resonate those divine qualities within these walls and all around this dwelling place. On the grounds and in the air and within the molecules that hold the spaces within these rooms.

Make of this dwelling a fortress of Spirit. Make of this dwelling a palace where perfection is mirrored. Make of this dwelling a living temple of Light. Anoint this house with the vibration of higher heaven. Let those who come feel the presence of Angels within this place. Let them feel the thirst of the heart for True Love. And let it be the inclination within these walls to come closer and closer to Truth and Unity.

Angel, stand at the door and softly greet all who enter, bringing each one into resonance with the comfort of the Deep Self. Establish platinum nets of protection in the doors and windows. Amen

For the Safety of Animals

I invoke the presence and love of Mother Earth, the Angel of this House, the Angels and Nature Spirits who guard this land on which I live, and the Higher Selves of the predators who live around us. I also call forth the protection of Archangel Michael and his legions of Angels and ask that a ring-pass-not of blue light be situated around my house and around my pets to protect them from any harm.

Angel of the House, please see that a protective grid surrounds the house at all times so that the animals residing here are protected from the wilder animals with whom we share this land.

Nature Spirits, please carry my love to the animal kingdom who dwell in this geographical area, yet help them to know that they are not to consider my family as food.

To the Higher Selves of the predators, I send my love and blessings. I bless you and send you love from my heart and wishes for your fulfillment; but I request that you find health and fulfillment in places other than our immediate domain. I am a guardian to the pets who live with me and I seek their protection from any violence. Amen

−8−

Healing the Earth

*I*n our growth, we have come to experience the Earth as a conscious being who undergoes Her own transformation, ascension, and healing. As our consciousness expands, we begin to truly see Her as Sacred Mother/Gaia/Mother Earth. As we heal ourselves, it becomes a natural urge to heal She who has supported us and supplied us with a home for our physical embodiments. In our conscious journey, we become interactive with Her and recognize that we have a responsibility and a relationship with Her. As we awaken to ourselves as guardians of Her Gardens, we feel that She is integral in our purpose. As we heal ourselves, we heal Her. As our auras are healed, so is Her atmosphere. As we transform ourselves, so is She transformed. And as we evolve spiritually, we become Her loving caretakers.

It is a natural progression in our own healing that the Earth be healed. As we open up to Her, we can talk with Her, feel Her, listen to Her, and be shown how it is that we can share in Her healing. Her healing is very important for She is preparing for Her next step, too. As She takes Her next step, the entire solar system becomes poised for its ensuing stage of growth. We see the thread of oneness in all actions, great or small, and the implications are great.

Nature Spirits

This is an invocation to Joy, to Splendor and to Balance. To the fairies, gnomes, elves and Nature Spirits who play in the grasses behind the flowers. Who frolic in the hills. Who would bring those gales of laughter, those somersaults of energetic balance to those of us who get so serious in our work and in our play.

Let this be an invocation for communion with our brothers and sisters who balance and restore nature. To put aside our notions of age and social pressures and social responsibilities and images and identities. To place our bodies and our hearts and minds upon the body of Earth and breathe with her. To follow the travels of a bug down a leaf. And place our arms around a tree. And ask a dog to take a walk with us as our friend, as our companion. And notice the day through the eyes, ears and nose of that great creature.

Nature Spirits, come forth now and enlighten my heart. Make me laugh. Tug at my hair. Pull me down in the grass and tickle my nose. Do what it takes when I hold the grim posture of imbalanced responsibility.

Respond to me, dear Nature Spirits. Send to me the flavor of the apple that hangs on the tree. Send forth on the wind the fragrance of the petal. Awaken my childlike delight, my childlike wonder. Let the spirits in the ocean dance upon the water. Let me forget the hour and remember the glory. Let me forget how cold the water is and feel the refreshment between my toes. Help me to sit down in the sand and water, and let my body sink into the elements and be in awe and be in wonder. And feel and feel and feel. Let me be open to nature.

Help me, Spirits of the air. Help me, Spirits of grace and beauty in nature. Draw my attention to the smallest ones, to the vibrations of love that underlie this creation. Amen.

Whales and Dolphins— Guardians of Earth

I call to the Whales in the oceans of Earth and salute their energy of Song that blesses all life. You who maintain the biosphere of this Great Planet through the living symphony of your music. You who are the guardians of the Earth Garden. You who sustain life on Earth, on land and in the sea. I invoke the dearness of your hearts to link with our human hearts. To work with us and speak to us and help us pick up our own guardian mantles and be the land guardians for Lady Gaia (Earth).

Assist us in our process of ascension and guardianship of our planet. Know that we thank you for carrying the whole Earth on your great backs. Inspire us, sing to us, and bring us forward into the new light of this great unfolding time. Wash over us with your playful passion and great fortitude and resonate to us your unending compassion and quiet commitment.

We invite you to become our friends. We invite you into our dream state at night and into *our daily meditations. We urge you to take a look upon the shore and find us there.*

Merge your song with our songs as we wake up to the Divine Plan for Earth. Plant the eternal tunes in our consciousness and awaken us further. Help us to be your Brothers and Sisters in and of the Light.

To our Dolphin Family, we offer our hands across the waters in thanks for your joy and guardianship, as well as your interaction with the food chains that sustain our lives. Let us see you dancing under the sea and leaping into the air. Come and know us and show us how to love!

We honor you and ask for your gentle lessons and messages to enter our consciousness. Help us to become the stewards of Earth to resume our responsibility as guardians of The Garden. Amen

For the Body of Earth and Our Bodies

I invoke the Light that makes all things in Creation. I call the Light through the inter-dimensional portals to Earth and into our Bodies.

O Light, pour forth now into this temple and resurrect it into the Everlasting Light of Immortal Consciousness.Lift this matter into the Light that knows no death, no birth. Lift density from this form and move my beingness into my Higher Ascended Body of Light that awaits me.

O Light, come now forth upon the face of Earth, into Her heart, into all the kingdoms and all the reaches of Her great Body. Alter Her vibration from the depths of Her great oceans to the tops of her great mountain ranges. Penetrate Her fields, Her flowers, Her animals, Her minerals and Her plant kingdoms. Sweeten the air surrounding Her body.

O Light, bring us into the Higher Realms. Carry us up the Ascension Ladder. Come now into our world full force, and bring us into our legacy, the legacy of Light from Our Father's and Mother's Great Mansion. Amen

Material Abundance

I invoke the Goddess Lakshmi, the Council of Prosperity for Earth and the guidance of St. Germain, carrier of the Freedom Flame, to bring forth energies to ascending Earth for the purpose of Her people receiving God's Limitless Abundance as expressed through the energy of money. I invoke this within Free Will and in accordance with the Divine Plan for Planet Earth and for each of Her citizens.

I ask that my Light and Love be added with blessings to the Thoughtform of Freedom From Financial Strain. I call the Violet Flame of Transmutation in, through, and around the atmosphere of Earth and direct it, as a Child of God into the heart of the governments and peoples of all nations to dispel thoughtforms of fear, greed, control, unworthiness, lack and limitation.

I join with Beings of Light and Galactic Agents of Change to replace these thoughtforms with Love, Common Union, Sharing, and Abundance. I ask that all institutions and agencies that handle or distribute funds be cleansed and purified by this Flame. And I request that this transformation happen as quickly and smoothly as possible.

Let the energies of Preparation for Transformation enter now and prepare the hearts and minds of human beings for financial freedom.

I ask for all the assistance and guidance that the Angels and Masters can give to remove the discord and power struggle inherent in economic systems presently on Earth. In accordance with the Highest Good, I call for destruction of the pattern of haves and have-nots. Let all who wish experience financial abundance and freedom from worry, struggle, competition, hunger, and lack of any kind. I ask that this happen in the Eternal Now in the name of God if this is appropriate for the Highest Good of each one. Amen

Invocation to
Mother Earth

Beloved Mother, I call upon You to carry
forth the Earth trail of my tears and fling them
across the Cosmic sky. Let them float lightly as a
rainbow mist sprinkling Your body, as my heart
takes flight.

Take my laughter and touch it with True
Mirth. Lace this laughter with the currents of Joy
of the Ninth Ray and let that Joy echo in Your
Mountains. May Your sweet clouds spin rapture
onto the Cosmic Highways ringing the Names of
the Beloveds across the Eternal Sky.

I call to the Entire Company of Heaven, to
all Masters and all Angels, and to the Silent
Watcher and Solar Guardians watching over
You: to unite the radiance of Your citizens and all
planetary activity of Light with the radiance of
the Heavenly Realms and all cosmic activity of
Light.

I call for a gathering of Love uniting The
Above with The Below on Your Surface to
empower You, cleanse You, anchor Divine Music

and Geometries into Your chakras, infuse You with Higher Frequencies, vivify Your atmosphere, restore the sparkle to Your waters, and lift remaining clouds of confusion and disharmony. I call for an immaculate concept of purity to wash over the 5 elements that work with You. May the Directors of the Elements of Earth, Fire, Water, Air and the Ethers be restored and bring resurrection and peace to the elementals working in Your gardens, Your land, Your oceans and Your air.

I ask for a special blessing from Earth's Planetary President Lord Buddha, and from Lord Maitreya who heads the Spiritual Hierarchy for Earth. I also ask for the blessing of Earth's Solar Presidents—Helios and Vesta—who hold the entire solar system in their solar heart.

You are my Earthly Home and I gratefully share my blessings with You. Amen

–9–

Celebrations & Special Occasions

*B*ehind every celebration is a sacred ceremony calling attention to the life within each hour, to the specialness of life lived in awareness. Celebrations focus attention on remembrance and as we reach for enlightenment and ascension, we honor remembrance as a key to understanding, appreciating, releasing, and evolving. It is our hope to remember who and what we truly are and to commemorate the sacred journey of Spirit into Matter and then Matter into Light.

Behind every celebration of a birth day is an awareness of what birth is, what we have been born into, where we have come from, and what it means. Behind every celebration of a marriage is the inherent understanding of commitment, love, true relationship, and union. Special occasions offer a vacation from daily living and a chance to concentrate on giving thanks or blessings. As we evolve in consciousness more and more moments become "special" and every hour, day, and moment becomes a celebration of the fullness that we feel. Celebrations of the life flowing through us.

Indeed, when we invoke higher love and awareness at particular times, we are asking for preparation for the time coming when all days are days of Christ awareness, thanksgiving, union, and rebirth. May all days become Holy Days!

For a Birth

In anticipation of this one's birth into form, I invoke the welcoming essence of Angels and Beings of Light to assist in the Birth Process. I ask to be overlit by Kwan Yin, patroness of women and birth, who ushers in Incoming Children. I ask for the beauty, balance, and grace of her presence to be with us.

I acknowledge the physical being assigned to this "new" lifestream and ask that if it is in accordance with the Highest Good, that this baby have easy passage into this dimension, and be blessed with radiant health and conscious awareness.

I call to the Ministering Angel who follows this Being from lifetime to lifetime and ask that the Ideal be Real for this Child of Light.

I ask for a blessing that this one come equipped with the gifts of the Holy Spirit and have strong use of the Light. Let this vibration add to the lifting of our world and all worlds. Let this child emerge in close association with the Higher Self and be Itself a Bringer of the Dawn of New Enlightenment.

I ask for health and vitality for the mother as she delivers new life/new consciousness as a gift to us all. Let this child know the self as a Son or Daughter of the One Most High. Let the personality be in awareness of the legacy of greatness that he/she carries. Amen

For a Marriage

On this day of Marriage, when you come together in love and unity, I invoke the Presence and wisdom of the I Am Presences of each of you to guide you both on the intersection of your paths of Light.

I call forth the Angels of the Pink Ray of Divine Love and Gratitude to bless this union. I call forth the Christ Energies to anoint this union with a Golden Rain of Light which will bring in the higher vibrations of completion and mastery.

I ask that this ceremony be overlit by an arch of Angels and be consecrated by an assembly of Masters of Light. Let the message of this ceremony be to know the goodness of togetherness as well as the worth of the individual. Let the two unite in a deeper commitment to end separation and to embrace Unity on all levels of Life.

On this day of Marriage, I invoke within you the seeds of Ascension, for within those seeds is the flowering of your inherent gifts and the unveiling of your true natures of Light.

On this Day I invoke a vision of another day coming when you shall marry your Christed Self.

When you two will dress up in your Light Bodies and come and take your places at the royal gate of Father/Mother God.

On this Day, you come together as a unit to increase the Light you hold. Take turns being the lit candle lighting the unlit candle. Retain your own Light as you ignite one another.

I invoke the Higher Selves of each of you to reflect your ancient past, your magnificent re-awakening, and your evolution into That Which You Truly Are.

I invoke a blessing for your home. May it reflect the part of you both that has never left your True Home. I call forth the Angel who will stand watch over your home and ask that it be protected from all discord. I request a blessing from Father/Mother God for this marriage. Let it become an outer expression of the Sacred Marriage of Divine Feminine/Divine Masculine within each of you. Let this coupling signify the linking of Form/Formless, Physical/Spiritual, Heaven/Earth, and Human/Divine within us all. May this Brother and this Sister be joined as a Son and a Daughter of God, here on Earth to help one another reach the highest potential in self and in each other. Amen

When Someone Dies

At this time of departure from the physical body, I invoke rivers of Peace to flow into the minds of those who would be in surprise or in bereavement. I ask that a bridge from the mind into the Heart be built by Angels who carry the deeper meaning of this experience.

I invoke the Angels of Death to stand guard and resonate the understanding of death as a passage into another dimensional aspect of Life and not the ending of Life. I invoke the Soul's wisdom which holds the secret of Life and Death. Let the Soul's remembrance stir through you now and flood your Beingness with conscious application of ancient memories retained in your heart. Let the process known as Death be known deep within you for what it IS and for what it IS NOT.

Let fear and remorse be no more. Instead let be created an understanding of this: the Spirit of the departed one is beginning a new Initiation which is cause for Celebration. Within the unfoldment into Oneness, we all grow towards unity. Unity holds inherent within it, the embrace of Re Union.

To the one who has left the body, let the door to the heart chamber fly open as your feet touch the gossamer ladder upon which you tread. May you ascend this ladder into Greater Wisdom and Understanding. May you see the fire letters PEACE that are written in golden rivulets of tranquility as you journey toward a fuller expression of self.

Release yourself now into the Love that lies ahead of you. Amen

At the Wesak Celebration

For eons, every year on the night of the Taurus moon the Cosmic Event called the Wesak Festival is celebrated as the holiest day of the year from the viewpoint of the Ascended Masters. Originally the celebration took place in the Wesak Valley in the Himalayas where those on pilgrimages had to find the chosen site with only the map of the heart. Today the holiday is celebrated and honored both in the East as well as in the West.

The high point of the event is the visitation of Lord Buddha who arrives in his luminous form to bless the human race with an outpouring of love and light commemorating the anniversary of his birth, his enlightenment, and his ascension or graduation from the school of Earth. He offers a benediction of Buddha Life Force to the entire planet, while those in attendance on the inner planes and those consciously aware of the occasion receive deep spiritual communion and spiritual renewal. Lord Buddha, who is the president of this planet, spiritually speaking, bestows ethereal substance from the Higher Realms into the atmosphere of Earth. One can prepare for the visitation in meditation and join with others in celebrations that take place globally.

The Wesak truly nourishes the souls of humankind for it is a celebration of Oneness. While it began in the

East, it is now becoming popular in the West for the intention of Wesak is to honor all paths to God, all traditions, all religions, all spiritual teachers, gurus, and truths. With Lord Maitreya, the Planetary Christ, playing an active part in the festivities, Wesak demonstrates the marriage of Christ and the Buddha, the East and the West, as well as Buddhic Wisdom and Christ Love.

Invocation at the Wesak Celebration

Beloved Buddha, I call you forth to bathe me in your golden gift. Help me to open my heart as full as the Taurus Moon in order to receive your blessings of love and light. Let my heart become a grail to carry back into my life the sacred water you offer in benediction.

I call forth a Wesak ascension activation at my highest potential. I ask that my mind be linked with the Wisdom of the Buddha and that my heart be touched by the Love of the Christ Please help me to let go of the differences between the Children of God and see how similar we are. Open my mind from all mind locks and help me to erase all obstacles from my path. Renew me with the promise of yet another year of service work and help me to serve freely, joyously, and completely.

Lord Buddha, I ask for your Rod of Initiation that I might begin the next level of initiation available to me at this time. Look upon me and within me and see my service potential. I wish to

come into closer communion with the entire
Spiritual Hierarchy.

Let me be the grateful recipient of an
imprinting of the Christ/Buddha Archetype to
replace my other archetypes.

Let the angels anchor Christ qualities and
Buddha virtues into my consciousness and four-
body system.

I request from all of the Masters and Angels
gathered at the Wesak forum, a showering of the
Light of 1000 Suns. Please shower upon me the
maximum amount of core love so that I can move
forward in my evolution and serve better.

From you, Lord Buddha, I ask for an
increase in my light and love quotients. I ask that
you flood every chakra, every chamber of every
chakra and each of the petals of each chakra with
the sacred water from your golden bowl of
blessings. Bless me deeply so that I may carry
your blessings back home with me and be a
conduit of love energy for everyone I meet. From
you, Lord Maitreya, I ask for a re-kindling of the
Christ I Am. As the Wesak ceremony laces
together all traditions and all paths to God,
please help me to be a shining example of
reverence for all life and acceptance for all

brotherhoods and sisterhoods of light in the new millennium. I am ready to renew my commitment to God and the Masters. I am ready to re-ignite my covenant with God to bring God back into the hearts of all the people of Earth. Give me the strength and the endurance to follow in your golden footsteps and to fluidly move into my enlightenment and ascension into the light.
Amen.

At Christmastime

At Christmas I invoke the love of Sananda
Jesus the Christ, Mother Mary, and Joseph (who
is Ascended Master St. Germain.) May it flow to
all who celebrate and be a reminder of the
rebirth of purity, love, and Christ action on
Earth.

I call forth the inner Christ that is in perfect
harmony with Father/Mother God. Let this day
honor the Christ child within who yearns for
birth, growth, and maturation. Let this day that
commemorates a holy birth, now celebrate
Ourselves as divine creatures living in human
bodies birthing Christ potential within us.

I call to my Christed Self and ask for it to
teach me self-mastery. Let the gifts that the three
wise men delivered, stand for my own gifts of
Love, Wisdom & Grace. Let me be wrapped in
the swaddling clothes of understanding, recognition of self, dedication, and remembrance of
Source. Wrap me in the folds of the garment of
light that is my true identity as a child of God
and let this day be a birth-day for my spirit.
Amen

At Eastertime

On this day of Easter I honor Jesus/Sananda
the Christ and Archangel/Mother Mary for their
parts in preparing the consciousness of Earth
citizens for the Aquarian Age. I call forth the
presences of these great beings to be with me in
this Easter hour. I hold the image of the Resurrection Flame and call forth Archangels Gabriel
and Hope to bring the energies of resurrection for
humanity and for myself into focus within a great
lens of Light. Let this day honor the action of
resurrection: let it be a recovery of abilities and
gifts that are not yet within our reach. Let the
energy of renewal of connection to Source be now
infused within each human heart.

I call to my Christ Self, asking that this
aspect of myself come into dominion over me
now. I ask that it be felt as a gentle wind lowering
into my crown chakra, filling my entire body
with the power, wisdom, and love of a Christ.
Bring into blossom the seeds that were planted so
long ago when resurrection and ascension were
demonstrated and seeded 2000 years ago. Let the
flow of Christ energy go out to all who choose to
inhabit their Christed Selves and be resurrected

into the glory and power that once was prevalent on the face of our dear Earth. Let the demonstration that Jesus performed 2000 years ago, be now understood and expanded so that all of humankind who choose can now understand our part in the blueprint he offered to the world. Let the example of his teachings and his ascension as well as the unconditional love and concentration of Mary be imprinted within each of us, so that we become the teachers we are, experiencing unconditional love and profound focus, and the command necessary to bring our bodies into the higher vibration that we call ascension.

May we all live our lives in the Posture of Blessing all life. Let us move into the compassionate heart—forgiving any who may have harmed us. Knowing only ignorance of the Divine Plan and ignoring God would and could result in harmfulness to a sister or a brother. Let be resurrected this thoughtform: we are all part of the Eternal Self. There is only One Ascension— the Ascension of God. Amen

An Invocation to Clear a Room or a Building

I invoke a clearing now of this (name place)
to clear all negative emotions and intentions that
are not in accordance with the vibration of love
and the remembrance of Source. I call for a
clearing of residual energy patterns that hang in
this room, left by disharmonious visitors and
discordant thoughtforms to this place.

I call forth the Angels and Masters that
would assist in the disassembling and the clearing
of any energies that are not of the Christed
vibration.

I call forth the Violet Flame to swirl through
this (name place) extinguishing discord and
replacing it with the sweet fragrance of peace,
harmony, and willingness to receive love. Violet
Flame, take this space which has been filled with
less than light, with less than Love and fill it now
with the properties of Love.

Archangel Chamuel, bring forth the love energies, the gratitude energies, the energies of openness and forgiveness.

Archangel Zadkiel, bring forth Violet Flame Angels to assist in escorting out discord and ushering in a Love that underlies all life and is within all living substance.

I invoke the full bursting forth of the Light that would enhance the brilliance and the sweetness of that which could dwell here. Let there be Light here! Let all who are not of the Light who would enter here, who would use whatever power they have to hide the love, to confuse, to distort—Let all leave now in the Name of God!!

Archangel Michael, place a wall of Blue Light and a Golden Dome of Protection around this dwelling place as a shield of protection. Escort from this (name place) all who would oppose the light. Show them the Light that they may go there now.

Lord Melchizedek, Lord Metatron and The Mahatma, we ask for the protection of platinum nets in all doors and windows.

I thank you all. So be it and so it is! Amen

We End with a Message from an Inner Plane Ascended Master

Let us pray to God Almighty.

> To the Divine Force living in all Life,
> expressing Itself in all dimensions. Let us pray to
> the seed within all, to the Father and the Mother
> of all, The Creator of all worlds and the sustainer
> of all Life. To the ocean from which you have
> come and the ocean to which you are now
> headed. Let us pray for peace. Let us pray to
> come fully into the Destiny and the Love that has
> been granted. Let us put ourselves as Brothers/
> Sisters before the Most High and ask to be lifted
> and accelerated, loved and nurtured, and
> granted the wisdom of completion.

CR

Start your days with such a prayer. And after the prayer, perhaps link in with the Angels and the Masters who have your respect and your love. Bring them around yourselves, Dear Ones. Perhaps there is some hesitancy on your part to see yourself in the glowing colors of divinity. Maybe you have a double standard. You have respect and honor for many and yet you do not bring that same honoring, that same genuine love and acceptance into your own being. I wish that you could feel the depth of your heart and know how integral you are a part of All That Is. You would then be able to move forward in your life with exuberance, with honor for yourself. And with a bit more happiness and more of a carefree nature.

You are all a little on the serious side. You hold on even as you try to let go. This is very common for your brethren on Earth. I would suggest that you begin to spend more time in that sanctuary within you where you could develop more of a feeling for who you are and how special and beautiful you are. Undefined by where you live. Undefined by who is in your immediate family. Undefined by your health and by your wealth. Undefined even by your wisdom, by your name, and by your age. And all other criteria that you use to define yourselves. Go and find the core of your being and bask in that vibration, that energy that you truly are. In the Perfection and Love that is You.

This is your awakening time. And your awakening cannot be on the outside, it must be on the inside. And then invoke US to help you. You take many steps and then you turn and discount your own steps. You bring doubt into your own mind where there is plenty already.

Align yourself with your Higher Nature. Begin the practice of reaching up and into your Bigger Self, your Grander Self. Fit that skin around you. Dress yourself in that suit and it will suit you much greater than what you are now wearing.

You all have so many questions. Let us bring your questions down into a simpler form. Let us ask you what do you know? What is your knowing? What do you know for sure? What do you hold within yourself that no one can take from you? What is it that you possess that cannot be robbed from you, that cannot be diluted, that cannot turn against you? What is it that you know is real? What is it that you depend on that is there day after day after day and in all the moments?

If the answer is an experience of Divine Love, a line to Source, a lifeline to the energy of All That Is, then you are privileged and fortunate and you are well on your way to becoming instrumental in the work that is at hand in transforming your planet, your brethren, and yourself.

And if that answer is not forthcoming with surety, with certainty, based upon a real experience, a deep knowingness that follows you wherever you go, then, Dear Ones, this is where you must start. And so what can you do to bring that certainty to you? For it is locked within you. All answers are within you. So discover how to get inside. Go into your own heart and if you call upon me, I will sit with you there.

—*Lord Sananda/Jesus the Christ*

Afterword

Who am I?
I am a God Being
I am the Creator in form

What Time is it?
Time to know myself as a God Being
Time to act as a God Being

What do I thirst for?
Love
Awareness
Perfection
Enlightenment
Ascension

Where do I belong?
Heaven on Earth

What do I say no to?
To limitation,
To unempowerment,

To lack,
To separation,
To death,
To the negative ego

Where was I born?
I was not born
I emerged from All That Is

What keeps me from my knowingness?
Misconceptions and fear-based programs
Forgetfulness
Separation
Misguided Thoughts
Judgments
Negative Ego Consciousness

Why am I here?
To master the Earth experience
To return to Source consciously
To make Divine the human experience
To master control of energy, thought and emotion
To know I am Spirit embodied
To Ascend into Higher Consciousness,
taking my body with me
To embrace the Christ in me; to become a Christ
To take this body into the Light

To wake up and pay attention
To take this Earth into the Light
To Know Myself
To Know the Oneness
To Love unconditionally
To know that I and Mother/Father God are One
To *be* the Power and the Glory that I AM

○3

What is Life?
Life is Light
Light is Love
Love is Energy
Energy is God.
God is consciousness
Consciousness is awareness of self
Self is God I AM
I AM Union
Life is Union

○3

Why invoke?
To strengthen myself
To awaken myself
To master myself
To create the highest good for myself and
for the Earth
To connect with Source
To become the I AM that I AM

About the Author

Wistancia Stone is an articulate and talented communicator, and former co-host of the TV show, *Bridging Heaven and Earth.* She is a telepathic voice channel for the inner plane planetary and cosmic Masters and Archangels, and a spiritual teacher. She specializes in ascension clearing, ascension activation, interdimensional journeying, and healing with Masters and Angels, meditation, and spiritual counseling. With twenty years of dedication to unfolding the spiritual path, she now designs personal invocations and meditations for others.

Wistancia lives with her husband, Dr. Joshua David Stone, founder of the Melchizedek Synthesis Light Ashram and Academy, in Los Angeles, California.

Sacred Space
for Your Personal
Invocations